On The Wings Of The Wind

By
Louise Scarmato

_____

On The Wings Of The Wind
Louise Scarmato

Published By Parables
April, 2021

All Rights Reserved. No part of this book may be reproduced or utilized in any form or by any means, electronic or mechanical, including photocopying, recording, or by any information storage and retrieval system, without permission in writing from the author.

    Printed in the United States of America

Readers should be aware that Internet Web sites offered as citations and/or sources for further information may have been changed or disappeared between the time this was written and the time it is read.

On The Wings Of The Wind

By
Louise Scarmato

TABLE OF CONTENTS

	Dedication	3
	Acknowledgement	5
	Introduction	11
1	**LIFE WORTH LIVING**	15
2	**BEYOND THE CHAOS**	21
3	**FREEDOM**	23
4	**A LIFE OF VIRTUE**	29
5	**DIVISION**	35
6	**TRUTH**	41
7	**IN PURSUIT OF TRUTH**	45
8	**A CALL TO ARMS**	51
9	**RUN YOUR RACE**	57
10	**METHOD OF CONTROL**	61
11	**THE IMPORTANCE OF LANGUAGE**	65
12	**WHAT IS A STRONGHOLD?**	71
13	**DISCERNMENT**	77
14	**STAY THE COURSE**	83
15	**THE VOICE OF TRUTH**	93
16	**TIME**	101

17	*SPIRITUAL WARFARE*	107
18	*HEAVENLY ASSISTANCE – ANGELS*	123
19	*FOLLOW THE LIGHT*	133
20	*OUR MOTHER IN HEAVEN*	139
21	*PLOT TWIST*	167
22	*DIVINE MERCY*	179
23	*FULL CIRCLE*	183
24	*WORDS OF ENCOURAGEMENT*	187
25	*YOU ARE THE HIDING PLACE FROM THE WIND*	194
26	*PERSONAL NOTES & FINAL THOUGHTS*	197

DEDICATION

This book was written for my daughters, Roxanne and Natalie, and my son-in-law's, Thomas and Brandon, and especially for my grandchildren, Thomas, Daniel, Derek, Alivia, and Justin.

As the winds begin to change, follow His Way to the Truth and To Life.

ASPIRATION

This book was written to give clarity to this present time. My hope and prayer is that I have most humbly executed this book to His Honor and Glory.

INSPIRATION

"…He mounted a cherub and flew borne on the wings of the wind…"
"...He reached out from on high and grasped me, he drew me out of the deep water…"
"…He set me free in the open, and rescued me, because he loves me."

Psalm 18: 11, 17, 20.

ON THE WINGS OF THE WIND

Wind of change – an influence or tendency that cannot be resisted.

"When they sow the wind, they shall reap the whirlwind."

Hosea 8: 7

"One who pays heed to the wind will not sow, and one who watches the clouds will never reap."

Ecclesiastes 11: 4

INTRODUCTION

As the winds begin to change, we are faced with a choice. What direction do we go? Do we just move forward to what was normal before, or face a new beginning into a new normal? Those who know the truth understand that such a time would call upon us to make a choice. The key is to follow the Truth, it will lead us to the Way, thus ordained by God.

If we place our faith and trust in Him, the winds will move us on a course that has been predestined since the beginning of time. Many believers are aware that His course is the only way toward joy, hope, freedom and peace – a life worth living. As spiritual beings, we know that He has foreseen the happenings in this world today and has provided a way for us to live a life worthy of His Promises. We will know the right way, when our feet are on the right path because a peace will settle within our souls. We will begin to move within our new space enlightened by the revelation that we are home, in a place of freedom. It will be the freedom to choose His way of life, and a remembrance of our history.

In this present time, we must never give up any ground that has already been won from the enemy. It is our God-given right to be able to freely worship and live-in freedom as true believers in God. It is in alignment with His Promise to us, as His children, to hold this truth alive in our hearts and minds. We must never relinquish any rights to our freedom, which is a pride for our country as Americans and a nation under God. We have only to reflect on our history to know how precious it is to maintain our liberties during turbulent times and against the enemy.

**"You never know how much you really believe anything until its truth or falsehood becomes a matter of life and death to you."
C. S. Lewis**

In the past and present time, many people have come to this country to live a life of freedom. Our country stands as a beacon of light for many people all over the world. Throughout time, so many heroic lives were lost just to preserve our freedoms. But now, in this time, the enemy has gained entrance within, it has infiltrated within the confines of our minds and hearts, and reached into our cities, states, country, and even the world. The evil one's agenda is to destroy the essence of all that is good, all that is sanctified by God as truth, whereby leading to the destruction of all humankind. It is a bending of your will, by the bending of your knee, to the subjugators who are waging war against us, hegemony. Hegemony is the "leadership or dominance, especially by one country or group over others; synonyms: dominance, power, supremacy etc." A plan that has been conjured up by evil with the intention to dominate us, and destroy all that we hold sacred. So, where do we go? What do we do?

LIFE WORTH LIVING

The beginning of a "life worth living" starts when you set your feet upon the path of truth; you will find a newfound place. It will become a sanctuary, a way of life, and the place to be in all its comfort and ease. There is freedom in such a place, to finally know that you are home, living out your purpose, and hopefully, fulfillment.

We were created for this time and space, hand-selected by God, with a mission. This time was set aside long ago by Our Creator and well-planned before we were ever born. Every movement well-orchestrated and synchronized to this exact moment in time. Our ideals and principles set into a foundation of faith, hope, and trust. Lo, and behold, we were born with a purpose.

Our heart should feel joy to such truth. Throughout many years, we have been inundated with life and its experiences and their effect upon us to ever believe that we have a purpose; better said that God has a purpose for each one of us. This realization is so profound in that "we all matter", maybe not in this world, but to another heavenly world. Our existence was not just a random event, but rather controlled by Our Supreme Being. We matter, what a revelation! We all matter, and all of us are born with a purpose. Every experience, choice, and interaction are carefully used to encourage us toward the road we should travel. That is why the choices that we make in our lives do matter. Throughout our journey, circumstances and events continuously happen, and life moves on, as we navigate toward or away from the path that we should follow in our lives. Again, it is our choices that determine if we are on the right path. Sometimes, we remain in a set pattern without a conscious thought to where we are going. Then, a major upset such as a "pandemic virus" hits the entire world. We are told to quarantine, put the brakes on and forced to stop. Time is given to look at life differently, from another perspective.

"We know that all things work for good for those who love God, who are called according to his purpose."
Romans 8: 28

It is now blatant to us what was allowed to infiltrate our society, and those placed in power and control over ourselves, families, and way of life. So much occurred while we were sleeping and moving forward on the treadmill of our lives. Now we are not only personally examining our position in a job, relationship, and finances in a different perspective, but scrutinizing the condition of our society, and most important, the fate of our spiritual well-being. Do we really want to return to "normal"? I was living normal for so long without a conscious thought to what was happening around me. Something was missing, no matter where I was, I lost any thought of purpose. This absence allowed my mind to recreate thoughts of how I wished life to be.

Was that normal? What is normal? Normal is what you tell yourself normal is, it's your story. Can't we make our own stories and if not, why not? Who told you that you can't? Be vigilant at this time to the term "new normal" being used to indoctrinate into our society. Definition of normal – conforming to a standard; usual, typical, or expected. We are spiritual beings, so by faith we can find our "new normal". We must follow His truth, and ignite the fire within, to be one with the Holy Spirit as the winds guide us toward His Way and to Life.

"The wind blows where it wills, and you can hear the sound it makes, but you do not know where it comes from or where it goes; so it is with everyone who is born of the Spirit."
John 3: 8

Three words entered my thoughts that I will share with you and use at a later time, but just reflect on their meaning - **mindfulness**, **sagacious**, and **discernment**.

Mindfulness – the quality or state of being conscious or aware of something. A mental state achieved by focusing one's awareness on the present moment, while calmly acknowledging and accepting one's feelings, thoughts, and bodily sensations, used as a therapeutic technique.

Sagacious – having or showing keen mental discernment and good judgment, shrewd. Sagac – wise, 17th century, clever, intelligent, insightful, thoughtful, discerning.

Discernment – the ability to judge well (in Christian contexts) perception in the absence of judgment with a view to obtaining spiritual direction and understanding.

(The New Webster Dictionary of the English Language, 1989, NY)

BEYOND THE CHAOS

This is a time to get beyond the chaos and examine our foundation. The substance of one's life is simple, it is in our faith. It's to truly know that God is with us. He is the Great I Am, Our Provider, Our Deliverer, Our Redeemer, and Our Restoration. He revives our soul, when asked, no matter what the circumstances. He is Our Source. He is always on our side.

We were created with a purpose and promise of fulfillment. We have an angel preparing the way to guide and protect us. As we move forward in the light, our path will be clear, and we will walk upon His Holy Ground. The ground prepared for us since the time of our creation. It awaits us. He is Merciful and Compassionate. He knows the challenges that we will face; He has always sent His angels in preparation to defeat our adversaries from within and without. Our adversaries are many from the outer world, and some are ingrained in our hearts and minds as strongholds. Strongholds can be our worst enemy, which halt the flow of graces and blessings that God desires to bestow upon us. We can defeat them only by the power of prayer and identifying them by name. (I will get into that later in the book.)

"I consider that the sufferings of this present time are as nothing compared with the glory to be revealed for us."
Romans 8: 18

FREEDOM

"Where the Spirit of the Lord is, there is freedom."
2 Corinthians 3:17

So, freedom is where we begin our new journey. A journey to the stars, it is the place that has been destined for us since the beginning of time. A place where truth is not overshadowed by lies; obscured of its meaning. It is our rightful inheritance by God to attain wisdom on the narrow road, which has been uniquely designed for His children to acquire freedom from conformity.

"Do not conform yourself to this age but be transformed by the renewal of your mind, that you may discern what is the will of God, what is good and pleasing and perfect."

Romans 12:2

In this present moment, you will be able to discern the will of God, and follow the path designed especially for you. But first, you must leave enough room in your mind, to be able to hear Him. We have so much clutter wrapped inside such a small space, our brain, which is condensed with the old thoughts and patterns, messages and clichés, that God's message can't infiltrate inside. Our thoughts are a mess, totally conditioned to hold negative feedback from ourselves and others. So how do we get rid of the clutter? It is simple, prayer removes all clutter, pray until all negative thoughts are gone. This is how you get rid of old patterns toward your thought behavior, you set a new pattern in prayer. Every time a thought enters your mind in negativity or a disruption of your peace, stop, don't entertain it, just go into prayer until it is gone. A new pattern will take shape and become a new way of thinking. Our human nature is designed to entertain every thought, it is no wonder that we can never find peace, or that peace is so easily disrupted during the course of our day. Remember, we are now creating a new normal, so let us begin to bind our mind to the mind of God and gain control of what we entertain in our thoughts, in order to gain peace.

In my last book, On the Frontlines, I went into much detail on how the Enemy attempts to disrupt our lives and cause havoc. The Enemy has new tactics and strategies in this present time. He is relying on the old ways, but he has much assistance from the outside chaotic world of today. My book delved into the many ways the enemy can predict the outcome of any adversarial confrontation provided by his world, others and ourselves. Now take us into the present time, "adversarial" is beyond our norm, and way of life. It has been deliberately displayed to offend our senses on every level, in order, for us to either ignore, or engage, either way it has a devastating effect on our minds. This method has been studied over time, and it is not the first time that it has been slowly infiltrated into a society. Our minds are forced to make a conscious decision on whether to resist or acclimate ourselves to their new normal or rise above with the truth. It is only through Our Almighty Father that we shall conquer this adversary. The divine revelation is that the war has been won, and it is victorious in God's favor. We are on the winning side. It is in the battle that we must continue to pray, and ask for His guidance, protection, and strength. It is through the battle that we will find ourselves as true warriors in God's army.

This is a war between good and evil. It is a war that has been going on for century after century. The enemy has stored up an arsenal of new research data which was established in the previous century.

The proverbial frog in the pot of lukewarm water, slowly raise the temperature, and before long the frog is boiled to death. Never to jump out of the pot, or without any awareness of the rising temperature. Acclimate is to "adapt". So over time, we have adapted to the escalation of lies and deceit and painted the world gray in color. No longer right or wrong, but gray with the premise that it can't be wrong if it celebrates choice, rights, or freedom for a group. Again, semantics used with ingenuity, and let us not forget "political correctness, identity politics, redefined semantics, cancel culture and the "mask". How obvious has this become, but yet it seems to be escaping our notice. So, we drudge along, and they await our resistance, and there is none. They hear crickets, maybe faint objections, but those small fires are extinguished quickly, because we are not gathering our hands together to pray for God's mercy, and to hold the line in truth. Never let go of the truth, Jesus Christ is the Way, the Truth, and the Life. Do not waver in your conviction instead gain your strength and courage from He who is always with you in every battle. Trust Him to take you through, and follow the Light, you will get to the other side in Glory. This is His Promise to His children, and He is Faithful and True to all of His Promises.

"So, whoever is in Christ is a new creation: the old things have passed away; behold, new things have come."
2 Corinthians 5:17

So, let us begin as a new creation in Jesus Christ and follow His Way to the Truth and to Life.

A LIFE OF VIRTUE

To Divide is to conquer, and that phrase is prevalent today in this time of chaos and confusion. Most of us get up in the morning and attempt to proceed with our same routine, in order, to feel normal. Most seem anesthetized to the fact that there is a heinous agenda to destroy our way of life. Evil has been infiltrating our society throughout the centuries, but now, in this present time, it has jacked up its efforts for total power and control. The plan is to not only diminish the light, but to obstruct it in every way. Evil has a stranglehold upon this world. However, it took time as it gained entrance by just a crack in the door and eased its way into our society little by little, until it burst the door wide open. Just a crack, that's all it needs, and evil has a foothold into our way of life. Now, it will take all of our Heavenly Christian virtues, combining the four classical cardinal virtues of prudence, justice, temperance, and courage (or fortitude) with the three theological virtues of faith, hope, and charity to defeat this enemy.

Virtue is a trait or quality that is deemed to be morally good, and thus is valued as a foundation of principle and good moral being.

Personal Virtues are characteristics valued as promoting collective and individual greatness. In other words, it is a behavior that shows high moral standards. Doing what is right and avoiding what is wrong. The opposite of virtue is vice.

Prudence – The ability to govern and discipline oneself by the use of reason, sagacious in the management of affairs, caution as to danger or risk. Synonyms – wisdom, judgment, foresight, discretion, forethought, care.

Justice – Moral rightness, the quality of being just.

Temperance – moderation in action, thought, or feeling restraint.

Courage – Strength in the face of pain or grief. Synonyms- bravery, fortitude, boldness, determination, daring, valor, fearlessness.

Faith – is believing God's promises, trusting in his faithfulness, and relying on God's character and faithfulness to act.

Hope – is the confident expectation of what God has promised and its strength is in His faithfulness.

Charity – in Christian thought, the highest form of love, signifying the reciprocal love between God and man that is made manifest in unselfish love of one's fellow man..

"The only reward of virtue is virtue."
Ralph Waldo Emerson

These virtues will aspire us to a higher moral standard to become a good moral being. The bar has been set to a very high level, but these times call for extreme measures. This is our prayer, and our request for each one of these virtues to become a quality or trait of our character. This is your new normal.

The new normal will require courage and the ability to speak the truth. The truth is being distorted and those who wish to bury the truth, become enraged when confronted with it.

Without truth, we will fall, and lose our freedom. It is our God-given freedom, which was attained, maintained, and retained by the blood and loss of lives by so many of our gallant, and courageous soldiers throughout many wars. This is the reason for eradicating history from the textbooks in school. When we read about past history, we become inspired by the experiences and struggles of those who rose to the challenges they faced against their freedoms. We must rise to meet our challenges in this present time. Knowledge of history is a powerful weapon if used with the right intent for the common good.

The importance of living a good life is to evolve overtime, not with someone else's thoughts, but our own.

We are not perfect, and each of us are in a constant struggle with our human nature. Our human nature is flawed, and that is the main reason why we need faith, hope, and trust in God. So, in this present time, we are faced with an evil calculated agenda to overthrow all our liberties, and rights that we hold so dear, and desire to hand-down to the future generations.

So, what is our next step? It is to seek the truth. We must be in alignment to truth, so we can hold onto our freedom. Those in authority start by taking freedom away a little at a time. They test the waters, if we yield to the first step, it continues onto the next, a slippery slope. Before you know it, all of our freedoms will be gone. Once lost, freedom is never given back, it has to be taken, a bigger battle. In this pandemic, we are more than capable of proceeding forward safely, and to act responsibly, without reprisals or fines, and the restrictions that are definitely questionable and irrational on every level. Reclaim your citizenship as a true believer in God, and country. United we stand, Divided we fall.

DIVISION

If your ultimate goal is to divide a people of a nation, you do so with the use of semantics and intimidation. First, the misuse of semantics is when you pick apart a word to draw a different conclusion, and insidiously, apply the meaning of the word in how it relates to other words or its subject. Perfect example is the Supreme Court hearing for a nominee when senators described the word "preference" regarding sexual "orientation" as "offensive and outdated". Immediately, late into that night, the Merriam-Webster Dictionary changed its definition of the word "preference". In September 2020, the dictionary had considered the "term interchangeable with "orientation." Due to the pressure on the left, the definition was altered. Now it will be offensive to use the term "preference" in such regard.

Even the definition of a vaccine was altered in the Merriam-Webster Dictionary. The definition of a vaccine is "a preparation of killed microorganisms, living attenuated organisms or living fully virulent organisms that is administered to produce or artificially increase immunity to a particular disease." They changed it to include: "a preparation of genetic material (such as a strand of synthesized messenger RNA) that is used by the cells of the body to produce an antigenic substance (such as a fragment of virus spike protein)".

    Confusing but well-used by those whose agenda is to promote a deterioration of our society. You can examine history to understand its determination to annihilate the truth by the use of semantics. They use language, and one-phonetic word or phrase to indoctrinate its use by repetitive means and association in the relationship to the meaning of a word. There is a great power in the tongue, it is also written in Scripture…

"Death and life are in the power of the tongue; those who make it a friend shall eat its fruit."

Proverbs 18:21

Words are carefully selected to assert its meaning to someone's agenda and sway public opinion. It's by association that we are indoctrinated with a new norm. Most whose agenda is to change society and void it of any rules but their own, will say this is progress, (progressive). Again, the frog, slowly they infiltrate with change, raising the heat from simmer, medium, and then high until the frog boils to death. In the chapters ahead, I will show examples of how the extremes in our society have reached the boiling point.

Freedom is precious, and we, as a nation, have held our ground throughout time to preserve our way of life. And we must continue to uphold our unalienable rights to liberty, justice and freedom for all people.

As Ronald Reagan said, "Freedom is never more than one generation away from extinction. We didn't pass it to our children in the bloodstream. It must be fought for, protected, and handed on for them to do the same."

This quote emphasizes the immense responsibility for every citizen to uphold their freedoms. It is in this time that our freedoms are being trampled upon by an evil agenda. For almost a century, it lied dormant for the proper time to unleash its wrath upon all humankind. It seemed to lie dormant, but in the background, it gradually infiltrated its agenda into our society. Today, it is blatantly casting its darkness for all to see, witness, and experience the evil intentions of such a movement. During the pandemic, fear was the driving force, and coupled with the loss of control, it enabled them to rear their ugly heads. What we have permitted by relinquishing control of our lives, is for those with limited power to use suppressive methods to keep us downtrodden. Travel ban, masks, social distancing, no opening of schools, churches and businesses lead to a destruction of life as we know it, and let us not forget the chaos that is taking place with its riots, looting, harassment, beatings, and killings. We are being played with to the highest degree of order and control. When did we become sheep and a non-thinking entity in this country? It is known that they always attempt to "test the waters" and lay the groundwork to evaluate how quickly we would give up our freedoms. The pandemic was the perfect excuse to initiate control tactics as the media and "science experts" were eliciting large doses of fear every day. There was a constant barrage of fear by every means of communication, and it was well-used in our times of isolation. How we obeyed the commands in our states to flatten the curve and not to overwhelm our hospitals and essential workers. It made sense at first, so we did as told and it was accomplished. Never before in history were healthy people quarantined, but we listened and obeyed. Even though, we are all aware of each of our state's leadership and their "limitations" on the knowledge of this virus, but yet, we still listened and obeyed. What example are we showing to our children, and grandchildren. I think we should all review our history and learn once again about the courageous men and women who gave this country its greatness on this earth. If we continue on this path, our freedoms will be stripped away little by little, and we will become the frog in the pot. This is not a time of complacency; it is a time to rise up to regain our liberties with faith and trust in God. If not, we will wake up one morning and all of our freedoms will be gone.

    Only in the pursuit of truth can we find His way and be set free. Our final destination is with God. And if we truly believe this, no fear will enter your heart and mind. You will know that He's Got This!

TRUTH

"In a time of deceit telling the truth is a revolutionary act."
George Orwell

What is truth? Can it be defined? How do we know the truth? Is it clear or obscured? Can we make something the truth with shades of gray and convince ourselves that it is the truth? Have we come so far from the truth that we can no longer identify it? What part enables us to identify with the truth? Is it faith? Then without faith in God can we ever find the truth. Is the truth innately within us, created and rooted into the very fibers of our heart and souls? Or does the mind enhance its meaning and true origin or further confuse our will to identify it? Does reason play a part in discovering truth? How do we know that we are living in the truth? Is truth universal or personalized? Does God instill the truth within us at the moment of conception? Jesus Christ says, "that I am the Way, the Truth, and the

Life." So, He is the only Way to the Truth and Life. And if so, what about the unbelievers, do they ever know the truth? Is it ingrained in them at the moment of conception like the believers? Or must they find their Way back to the Truth.

"So Pilate said to him, "Then you are a king?" Jesus answered, "You say I am a king. For this I was born and for this I came into the world, to testify to the truth. Everyone who belongs to the truth listens to my voice." Pilate said to him, "What is truth?"
     John 18: 37-38

Truth is defined as *"purity from falsehood"* "state or quality of being true, sincerity, integrity. Conformity to fact or reality; exact accordance with that which is, or has been, or shall be."

"The greatest homage we can pay to truth is to use it."
     Ralph Waldo Emerson

Without truth, there will be no foundation for a life worth living. Goodness, justice, righteousness and virtues swallowed up in the confines of an evil world of nothingness, and lies void of compassion and love. Dreams and hopes extinguished into the fires of the abyss. Cast away are all thoughts of positivity toward a better world. All that will remain is the desperate adhering to a world based on self-preservation at any cost. It is a dangerous road without the truth, because anything will have its place in our society, and nothing will be beyond its tentacles. You destroy the truth by the three A's:

Abase - to cast down, to reduce low, to depress, to throw or cast down, to degrade. (guilt and shame)

Abash – confusion by shame, to confuse or confound, as by exciting suddenly a consciousness of guilt, error, inferiority, etc. (anxiety)

Abate – to beat down, to overthrow, to cause to fail, to lessen, to diminish, to destroy in any matter. (condemnation)

"He willed to give us birth by the word of truth that we may be a kind of firstfruits of his creatures."
James 1: 18

Seek the truth to find your way to the road less traveled, in order to fulfill a life worthy of His Promises, which time could never diminish.

IN PURSUIT OF THE TRUTH

In all of our understanding of history, the truth has prevailed beyond all rationalization and reason. The facts are information used as evidence of existence. If the facts of history are annihilated, we lose an important function of our mind, memory. Memory is the faculty by which the mind stores and remembers information. The faculty of the mind is "an inherent mental or physical power, an aptitude of talent for doing something." Our educational institutions have taken our most precious commodity, our children, in the hope of dismantling our country and its principles. They have simultaneously taken them from critical thinking, which was their job, and what you willingly provided for by your tuition and indoctrinated your child for their agenda. They created a generation filled with vitriol against country, and even their parents and family. They searched for our "Achilles heel" and they found it, our children. The result is a generation of young people who are angry, and destructive, and at times display a brutal resistance to everything that constitutes goodness and justice. Indoctrination is "the process of teaching a person or group to accept a set of beliefs." What better way to process this method then every day in a school setting by a radical professor or teacher's curriculum? Hope was lost for them among the older generations, but not all, because those who secretly wish to eradicate the truth are cheering this agenda forward. Their resources are enabling organizations to rise against the foundations and moral standards of our Declaration of Independence and our Constitution, in order, to institute their power and control. Those with an agenda are desperate, and it shows in their words, actions, and behavior.

    Hypocrisy is blatant against the litmus test of truth. They no longer try to hide it, but arrogantly state their objectives in every situation. So, we must be lights in the darkness, at a time when so many people are scrambling in fear, and trepidation to the incessant images of violence displayed from the media outlets. This evil agenda has hijacked the air waves to reach us on a 24-hour basis. These desperate efforts will not prevail, because it underestimates the resilient spirit of the American people. We have a foundation that has been built on the truth, and a country founded on the blood of those whose inspirations and determinations were based on God's will and purpose for this nation. Our founding fathers knew the complexities of human nature, so they proceeded to institute every law and regulation to protect our alienable rights of freedom, thereby; providing a moral standard and a foundation on human rights in the **Declaration of Independence:**

"We hold these truths to be self-evident, that all men are created equal, that they are endowed by their Creator with certain unalienable Rights, that among these are Life, Liberty, and the pursuit of Happiness."

President Abraham Lincoln made the Declaration of Independence, not the Constitution, the "heart" of policies on human rights for the government and the high standard on which the United States principles must attain for all of its citizens. It is the "focal point" on which we stand as American citizens, and the Constitution the "backdrop" for our Republic.

Our vision for the future must be in correlation to the spiritual realm. In the spiritual realm, the vision for America has been ascertained throughout time and space. It is a nation under God which upholds all liberties and rights for all people. Our victory depends on each one of us to never forget our enormous history of perseverance and fortitude to uphold this constitution. If they are allowed to chip away our rights, any semblance of who we are, will be lost forever. If we lose, the world will follow suit, and that is the agenda of evil. The truth must be upheld in all situations, not in whispers, murmuring, complaining, or in the confines of your home, but out in the public square for all to hear and listen, we must never forget who we are. First and foremost, we are children of God, Americans, who are granted the privilege to live in a society established in freedom and justice, and the right to live in faith and hope for a better world. It is our rights as spiritual beings that we can never allow to be taken from us, or we will forfeit our privileges as children of God. This is our time to rise in faith, to constitute the rights that we so easily inherited throughout time. The evil forces are running out of time, so they are becoming emboldened and desperate in every attempt to destroy this world. This is not a time to remain disinterested, but rather, spiritually rise and pray earnestly for our country. In prayer, the spiritual forces will become stronger, and our faith impenetrable. It is important to note that battles are first fought in the spiritual realm before it reaches the earthly realm. So, pray without ceasing, and allow your light to shine into the heavenly realm to defeat this evil agenda. Truth must prevail at all costs to annihilate this destructive force of evil. Only in the pursuit of truth can we find the Way and be set free. Our final destination is with God. One must never sever our relationship with God but only to unite our will to His Will in reposition to our inheritance as His children.

A CALL TO ARMS

Each of us have been given the ability and talents to be part of the solution. We were given these traits from God, by God, and for God. It's an inner voice that transmits to us the wrongs that need to be righted. We must listen to that voice and become a light in the darkness.

"We have not received the spirit of the world but the Spirit that is from God, so that we may understand the things freely given us by God. And we speak about them not with words taught by human wisdom, but with words taught by the Spirit, describing spiritual realities in spiritual terms."
1 Corinthians 2:12

Some are led to believe that they have become inconsequential to this war that is taking place on American soil. No one is inconsequential, everyone has a role to play.

The lies of the enemy are always "that we don't matter". But we do in every battle, whether big or small. This belief is why we are at this point in history in our country, we believed the lies. Know your enemy and understand why it is imperative that your thoughts of insignificance are vital to his plans of destruction for our country. Listen to the Voice of Truth.

"What eye has not seen, and ear has not heard, and what has not entered the human heart, what God has prepared for those who love him."
1 Corinthians 2:9

It's important to realize that what you are witnessing today is not regressive but progressive, it is an evil plan by the enemy to destroy this country and the world. We have lost the truth, while the enemy was working feverishly to undermine every moral standard and norm. Its objective is to conform our minds to a depraved manner of thought. Its offensive policies have been adopted through the process of acclimation with persuasive words or phrases. It was a slippery slope, which gained momentum, and became a mudslide. I have written in my other books that we have lost "outrage". We have become desensitized to the most immoral behavior, actions, words and laws that anything can become a norm, and nothing is objectionable. Where is our outrage? How did we become so apathetic? Again, we have lost the truth. What does this loss signify for the future generations? How will we be examined in history? These thoughts should be pondered for its significance to each and every one of us in this present time. How do you stop a mudslide? It is stopped when the roots of the trees and plants are strong in its foundation, not dead from erosion. This allegory refers to our faith. The foundation and root have always been in our love of God, Jesus Christ, and our faith in believing that He is in charge of our lives. It is living in His truth and following His way that we will gain our place with Him. It seems simple, but it's not in a world where the accelerator is pressed down to an extreme and moving at a fast speed causing extra stress, and to wear out more quickly. We must look at the world and all about us through spiritual eyes. The ranting, raving, hatred, animosity and violence exhibited every day, 7 days a week and 24 hours, it's exhausting. Let's shut it off, and resume in prayer, meditate on God's Word, spend time with loved ones, helping others, and expressing kinds words or deeds to encourage others to move out of the darkness into the light. Combat the evil forces by not allowing them to infiltrate into our minds and hearts. We must replace evil with good, and place Jesus Christ as **our** barrier against the evil forces. Remember who you are, you are a child of God.

"You belong to God, children, and you have conquered them, for the one who is in you is greater than the one who is in the world."
1 John 4:4

"No weapon fashioned against you shall prevail; every tongue you shall prove false

that launches an accusation against you. This is the lot of the servants of the Lord, their vindication from me, says the Lord."
   Isaiah 54:17

   This is our battle, which will be recorded in history. Let it speak of valiant soldiers and courageous undertakings, so that will inspire future generations to march forward. Pray against the forces who wish to destroy all that we hold sacred, as children of God, and citizens of this country. The time is now, do not lose sight of your goal, run your race with endurance and perseverance.

   "Therefore, since we are surrounded by so great a cloud of witnesses, let us rid ourselves of every burden and sin that clings to us and persevere in running the race that lies before us while keeping our eyes fixed on Jesus, the leader and perfecter of faith."
   Hebrews 12: 1-2

RUN YOUR RACE

It is important to note that when one is preparing for a race, you must believe that you will win. It is confidently knowing that every preparation has been ascertained to one's capacity of both physical and mental capabilities, which will determine that one can and will reach the finish line. Without every aspect of checks and balances, one could never hope to achieve their ultimate goal. It is the preparation and determination combined with the will of intention that provides a guaranteed victory. This process is universal toward all people and goals. It is what determines a winner or loser. Right intentions combined with proper preparations. In saying all this, that is how we prepare to run our race; one must first believe that they can win.

"Only those who will risk going too far can possibly find out how far they can go."
T.S. Eliot

So, we strive for the goal, the finish line. Now, we must apply such rigorous preparation to our spiritual life. It is what constitutes our good intentions in achieving what is both vital and everlasting for one's soul.

In conformity, we exist not live, as uninspiring and tedious beings who lack both character and individuality, and are void of any human feelings and qualities. A life without substance, belief, and faith becomes aimless and withers away in the hopes of endless attempts to satisfy oneself. It is a mirage of sorts casting its web upon the mind's eye, therefore consuming itself upon illusive wants, needs, and desires. It is how to program the viewer with a daily dose of media, in order to influence and comply to illusive forms of social behavior and therefore, its standards of acceptability.

"A man (or woman) must consider what a rich realm he abdicates when he becomes a conformist."
Ralph Waldo Emerson

In faith, we are taught to never fall into the perils of conformity, but to keep viewing a different world from a spiritual perspective. In faith, we combine both worlds, without faith, it is just this earthly world.

In **The Prayer of Jesus in John 17: 16-19**, it speaks to the heart of all believers.

"They do not belong to the world any more than I belong to the world. Consecrate them in the truth. Your word is truth. As you sent me into the world, so I sent them into the world. And I consecrate myself for them, so that they also may be consecrated in truth."

Consecrate is to "make or declare sacred, devote or dedicate formally and exclusively to a divine purpose."

METHOD OF CONTROL

It is important to begin this topic by reminiscing the days of old, BPC (before political correctness). It was a time of great thinkers, debaters, theorists, inventors, poets, writers, and just every day average intelligent people. Most unique in their thought process to evaluate a situation and express their reason why they interpreted a subject, book, poem, person, social and political viewpoint from their perspective. It was a time of critical thinking, and the pursuit was always for the discovery of the truth. This process would stimulate both the mind and heart to reach conclusions that brought value or knowledge about human nature, and its behavior and conditions. Our favorite and most memorable time was in the classroom in school, where discussions or debates would allow students to respectably agree or disagree with another's viewpoint. It challenged our minds to think, reason, and gain a broader multi-faceted knowledge on any subject or topic in our academic learning process. It was a grand time for learning, we were thinkers. Today, all that has been eradicated from most high schools and universities, these educational systems have been dominated by those whose desire is to change and distort all subjects of learning including the history of our country and its people. It began in 1960's when teachers in many American cities were given a handbook on how to taint our Western Civilization with every -ism and obliterate our principles and our identity as Americans. And sadly, they have even infiltrated the minds of the younger children in grade school.

"Education is a weapon whose effects depend on who holds it in his hands and at whom it is aimed."
Joseph Stalin

Young adults and children with a strong foundation will survive this indoctrination fed by the teachers and professors, but some will not. So, why was this allowed to happen, and why did we place the control into their hands without any objections? These are our children, not the property of the government.

"A nation never falls but by suicide."
Ralph Waldo Emerson

In George Orwell's book **1984**, the author wrote about an imaginary world to understand the effects of a totalitarian society, and the method used to subjugate the people held in its grip of power and control. It is a horrific adaptation of how citizens are forced to succumb to the tentacles of evil for their plan of destruction of a civilization and humankind. Orwell focuses on the mind as a means for them to gain their control. He applies the use of psychology that is most effective to both the conscious and unconscious thought and behavior of human nature to annihilate all positive values in a civilized world. What is most effective is their use of cruelty and torture to bring about their "purity" of thought. Orwell believed that if language could change for the worse, then truth could change into lies. This belief brings me to the present time in our society. In the book **1984**, there are two words that should cause a level of concern for most of us. The first word is Newspeak. Newspeak is a controlled language of limited vocabulary to reduce the capacity of human thought. The second word is Doublethink which is basically the power of holding two contradictory beliefs in one's mind simultaneously and accepting both of them.

Today political correctness is used to control language. Who constitutes what is politically correct? When did this come into our society as a norm to be used against others? Machiavelli argued that language is the key to the mastery of consciousness – a mastery more secure than anything that force alone can achieve.

THE IMPORTANCE OF LANGUAGE

Eyes to see, ears to hear is where we should be at this time void of all deception. It is by the use of discernment that we will find the truth. It is our goal as spiritual beings to seek the truth.

"Son of man, you live in the midst of a rebellious house; they have eyes to see but do not see, and ears to hear but do not hear, for they are a rebellious house."
Ezekiel 12:2

In Orwell's **1984,** it states, **"The Party told you to reject the evidence of your eyes and ears. It was their final, most essential command."**

Again, I reiterant, seek the Truth. The process is to control your language which will evolve into doublethink and control your sense of reality. Never allowing you to consciously think too deeply on one subject, therefore, intimidating, not convincing you toward their way of thinking. This process of alteration has been used before in the past, whereby, history books are revised, or parts eliminated to meet an agenda. In Orwell's 1984, it states that "Past events has not objective existence but survive only in written records and in human memories. It is said that if we are ignorant of history, history will repeat itself." So, evidently, ignorance is not bliss, but, rather dangerous in the future plight of this world. Political correctness is suffocating our thought process and enabling those who believe that they are in control, to harness any thought to rebel or revolt against their oppressive agenda.

    The belief is that there are more of them than us. That is a Saul Alinsky rule for radicalism, it is "Power is not only what you have but what the enemy thinks you have." He was a community organizer whose dedication page acknowledges Lucifer, the original radical who gained his own kingdom. So, knowing that, your choice should be clear, his agenda is evil and infiltrated into most of our institutions by those whose intentions are to destroy the fabric of our country. This information is not difficult to peruse, if one is seeking the truth. This evil agenda has been in place for more than a century in this country. Its goal is to destroy humankind and suppress all virtues through hopelessness and despair. Evil hates goodness, justice, unity, and freedom. It thrives on greed, hate, violence, disunity, and bondage. Evil is deeply rooted in its objective to gain power and control, so as to overturn and then, annihilate what Our Savior Jesus Christ came to earth, lived, died, and resurrected for all of humankind. He is Love, Joy, Peace, Hope, Justice, and Freedom. He is the Truth, and the Truth has set us free. We are redeemed, made whole, and deeply rooted in our faith to know who is in control of our lives. It is why we were created by Our Creator. There is no power greater than His. So, we continue on our journey living in faith, hope and the foundation that made us one of His. Live your life worthy to be called one of His children by following His Way, and His Truth, so that others may witness the glorious message of Our Savior.

"**What you do speaks so loudly that I cannot hear what you say."**
Ralph Waldo Emerson

We must lead by example through our actions and never sway from His truth and teachings, or we will enter their world of complacency and lies and be forever lost. Fear circulates continuously to entangle us in their consuming information of dismal foreboding. When we are afraid, we reach out for the familiar. There is comfort in the familiar, even though, it might be killing you. We live in a secular world where stagnant information and lies are fed to us on a daily basis. As human beings, we feel that we have a need to know this information. So, we continuously place our focus on the present-day news and experience a loss of control. When we feel out of control, it sets the stage for all kinds of negative emotions to envelope our well-being such as anxiety, depression, anger, hopelessness, etc. Our focus should be on faith, and our awareness that only God is in control of our future. This is attained through **mindfulness** and **discernment**. By being mindful, as human beings, on the mental, physical, and emotional levels, we can undergo a process which enables us to sever old thought patterns and repetitious forms of behavior, which has become second nature to us, strongholds.

WHAT IS A STRONGHOLD?

In the beginning of the book, I defined the word "mindfulness". To be mindful, one has to focus on the present moment and be aware of all feelings and thoughts and how one's body is reacting in their current state of mind. Most of us live in a reactive mode toward any stimuli, whether positive or negative, in a patterned response. This pattern was developed in our brain through neural pathways in our lives. Our lives encompass many circumstances and events where you were forced to respond due to fear, pain, disappointment, guilt, shame, judgment, anger, etc. in a negative way in order to protect oneself. It was a spontaneous response at first, and then after being used time and time again, it created a conditioned response without a thought to a similar circumstance in the past. We become conditioned and those responses become a part of our automatic reaction to any time we feel threatened or mistreated. It then becomes a stronghold without any conscious agreement.

We are no longer in charge of our feelings; we have lost control. Even though we have a capacity to reason; we are incapable to assess why our reactive response lead to a negative outcome. We can't question our behavior, and even if we do, our ability to reason has been compromised and one is left with the daunting realization that you had no choice. The outcome is always the same, the feelings leave us bewildered and confused and out of control.

Conditioning of the mind happens when we feel threatened or attacked. It doesn't mean that it has to always be dire, it could also come from an argument, opinion, or a slight attack of some sort. Strongholds are subtle and reassure us that we are justified because those pathways have been paved, seeded, and tended to for a long time. We are never in control when we respond from a stronghold. Even the definition of insanity won't apply, which is "to do the same thing over and over again and expect a different result." Again, we can't reason even the definition of insanity against a stronghold. We have altered our ability to penetrate the pathway to automatic responses because awareness has been lost. It is our strongholds that create so much havoc in our lives. What is a stronghold? A stronghold is "a place that has been fortified so as to protect it against attack; a place where a particular cause or belief is strongly defended or upheld." Many believers who are aware of the Enemy's agenda believe that the disruptions and eruptions in our lives are being orchestrated by the evil side. This belief is a possibility, but all the Enemy has to do is create the circumstance because he already knows our response. It has been observed and executed for many years, and the after affects are numerous. In those reactive times, we are void of grace, dignity, and yes, joy. We represent ourselves as angry and critical human beings. It robs us of our peace. One is left with feelings of sadness, and restlessness in emotion, and so dejected from your true self. It takes great effort to rise again and to feel better about yourself in your eyes, but mostly in God's eyes. It is a cycle unconsciously derived by the exact precision of intent to take away your control and your ability to reason. To overturn it, takes your will and mind to be united with God.

Memory plays an important role to creating a stronghold. That is why forgiveness is so important for us in order to live a life of freedom. Forgiveness is why Jesus Christ came in the flesh and was crucified for us. Our lack of forgiveness remains in our memory as an event that blocks our reasoning ability to be in control. It sits in our memory bank and recreates the same feelings and emotions, thus dragging us back to how it made us feel in the past. And on and on it goes, replaying the same scenario with the same outcome. So, we pray and ask for God's help and wonder why we are still feeling the same way. A vicious cycle for anyone who only wishes to be at peace. Strongholds are hell-bent on ruining our lives and causing such discomfort and pain, and seem almost impossible to be rid of, but "Nothing is impossible with God" Luke 1:37, He is not your circumstance, He is your Source.

Strongholds can also be passed down from one generation to another, generational strongholds. We can inherit a stronghold, which is a form of bondage or curse from those in our family lineage. As believers, we must remain focused and vigilant on our negative thoughts and behavior. It is imperative that you discern and reflect upon any or all influences passed down from one generation to another, whether biologically, socially, emotionally, psychologically, and spiritually as you ask for His divine deliverance. This is achieved through prayer. Prayer will free the mind and shut down all patterns of thoughts and behavior contrary to God's will for your life. In the power of His Word, all confusion, lies and deception can be removed from you and future generations. It is your conviction as a believer, to "stand in the gap" for your loved ones.

Prayer
Heavenly Father in the Name of Jesus Christ, I crush, smash, and destroy bondages and curses of any kind made at any point between generations. I destroy them right here, right now. They will not bind and curse any more members of my

family. I bind and loose these things in Christ Jesus Holy Name. He has given me the Keys and the authority to do so. Amen.
(Christian Ministries, Prayers)

Standing on His Word, you will be set free:

"I will give you the keys to the kingdom of heaven. Whatever you bind on earth shall be bound in heaven, and whatever you loose on earth shall be loosed in heaven."
Matthew 16: 19

Your prayer should be to loose peace, love, hope, joy, freedom, self-control and an abundance of blessings upon yourself and family on earth as it is in heaven. Be the one to "stand in the gap" and stop the transmission of generational strongholds from reaching future generations.

DISCERNMENT

Through the process of thought, we are changing the structure of our brains. Our brain is separate from our mind. This is the reason why we must control our mind thoughts, and way of thinking, so we can change the brain. In the Christian context, the definition of discernment is "perception in the absence of judgment with a view to obtaining spiritual guidance and understanding." In the dictionary, the synonyms for discernment – "insight, enlightenment, perception, sagacity, acumen, wisdom, intelligence, refinement, astuteness, sharpness, ingeniousness, judgment, awareness, etc." In our prayers, we must ask God for the gift of discernment. This is a valuable gift in these present times. In **1984**, George Orwell gives us the word Doublethink and defines its meaning. "The Essential Act of Doublethink is to tell deliberate lies while genuinely believing in them to forget any fact that has become inconvenient and then when it becomes necessary again, to draw it back from oblivion for just so long as it is needed to deny the existence of objective reality and all the while to take account of the reality which one denies – all this indispensably necessary." Ponder that statement for a while, it does take time to comprehend its meaning, but when it does clarity will return. Doublethink is to diminish the range of thought by altering or eliminating language, the end results is the denial of the truth.

"The further a society drifts from truth the more it will hate those that speak it."
George Orwell

"Make the lie big. Make it simple. Keep saying it and eventually they will believe it."
Adolf Hitler

Our main objective is to be aware of just what is filling our minds. Thoughts become part of the process to think, and hopefully, discern what we are thinking about in that moment. It is so difficult to discern our thoughts because they randomly fill our minds on a daily basis. Thoughts can affect our moods, and cause physical, mental, emotional and behavioral changes within us, and even sicknesses and diseases. What thoughts we allow to reside in our minds, create the way we think and feel about ourselves. It is important to become aware of what you are thinking about, and ask yourself if it is true.

Discernment is a gift to accept a thought as truth, or discard it as a lie. Only through faith, can you detoxify your thought process. For example, what was I thinking about when my mood changed to a negative mode? It's important to think about what you are thinking about, and then, process it for validity, and then, change it to a positive thought. Our spirit is strong to be able to discern the truth and transform all negative thoughts into positive thoughts. As spiritual beings, we draw the divine energy of God into the way we think and believe into our mind, heart, and body.

Our belief in God is dangerous to their agenda that is why they do all in their power to mock, denigrate, or oppose any one who is faith based in all areas of government and society. Faith allows an individual to rise above the noise and distractions of a secular world. It places your thoughts in conjunction to another world with divine intervention. You are never alone when you ask God for assistance. We must first surrender our will to God's Will and then, bind our minds to God's mind. In doing this, we become blank slates in our thoughts. It allows God to speak to us because we are now listening. If our mind thoughts are filling every portion of our brain, there isn't any room for God to fill us with His teachings, and enlighten us in times of need. Again, discernment is needed in times of turmoil. If not, we become filled with a thought pattern of the worst scenario bearing its weight upon us in hopelessness, and despair. We must focus upon what we are thinking about. Be aware and vigilant to transpire to rise above the distractions. It is the only way to prevail and reach a higher level of consciousness and be able to discern that you are in control of your thoughts. It is the one place where the mind can find peace, and over time, wisdom. This process is only attainable through prayer. Prayer will free the mind and place all thoughts in perspective and prioritize its importance to you in maintaining peace. It seems like a never-ending cycle, but once mastered, not a thought of negativity, worry, dismay, sadness, shame or guilt can take root.

Most important, we must rely upon Scripture. The Word of God can be used to wield its sharp, double-edged sword to cut down all negative words and deeds in your path. For example, the slingshot and stone used by David to take down Goliath. Like the giant, what you are facing becomes monumental in your mind's eye. The more you worry about a problem the more fear takes occupancy in your mind. It is a pattern that has been used since the beginning of time because it plays and preys upon our human nature. Who told you that you must be happy every day, and never have any problems? This is life, and as Scott Peck wrote in the first line of his book **The Road Less Traveled,** "Life is difficult." Throughout our life's journey on this earth, our only source is God. As we watch a world gone mad in its attempt to destroy all that we have valued, we must cling to our faith. Evil is drunk on power and wickedness to achieve its evil end. But always remember that we are never alone. God watches, He protects, He sees ahead, He comforts, and He restores. That is Our God, Our Savior Jesus Christ, King of Kings, and King of All Creation. So, as the world is running amuck, know that His Plan will take us through from this present time to eternity. It seems simple and it is, our faith and prayers will sustain us, and his protection will keep us safe. In this war against the enemy, we have Jesus Christ who is Faithful and True, and the Father of Mercies, and He is more than enough, El Shaddai.

STAY THE COURSE

**"Let your eyes look directly forward, and your gaze be straight before you."
Proverbs 4:25**

Change takes time. When you are in the process of trying to change the structure of your brain, and control your mind thoughts, be kind to yourself. Stay focused, but understand that it has taken many years to build these habits of behavior. There is always a situation or circumstances which attempts to take you back to previous strongholds with its patterns of thinking and behaving, but never lose hope. You must continue to go to the only Source, God. Consistency and perseverance during this time is prevalent in this battle. Sometimes, an activity such as praying, exercise, music, writing, meditating, walking, or just talking to a close friend, can relieve the angst, and clear your head. Some of our pattern of thinking is deeply rooted, and difficult to uproot. You can try visualizing Jesus standing before you, walking on the water, urging you on, as you fix your gaze on Him. Stay the course, as He assures you that you can do this. Miracles happen when we truly believe that He is Our Rescuer.

We live in an ambivalent world that changes course on a whim. Ideals, values, beliefs, opinions, circumstances etc. seem to change by each passing day. It could leave you jolted, unsure, insecure, but yet, you can live in contradiction to the world around you. He never changes.

"Jesus is the same yesterday, today, and forever."
Hebrew 13: 8

All of His Words are a contradiction to the logic and reasoning of this world. So, some may say that you are out of your mind to believe that He, Jesus Christ, Your Savior, The Redeemer of the World, is looking down and cares about your problems. There are times when being out of your mind, and silencing your thoughts can be beneficial. It is our faith, and His Word that tells us, YES, He does care about each one of us and our problems. He will give us the strength to persevere, provided that we have faith and trust in Him. This is one of the biggest character builders given by God, that we trust and hold on to our faith, as we wait for an answer to our problems.

"Ask and it will be given to you; seek and you will find; knock and the door will be opened to you. For everyone who asks, receives; and the one who seeks, finds; and to the one who knocks, the door will be opened."
Matthew 7: 7-9

When we are going through a difficult time, the minutes, hours, days, months, and years drag on, and cause a strain on your mind and heart. That is why the word "strain" is used in the Bible when we are urged to keep moving forward.

"Just one thing: forgetting what lies behind but straining forward to what lies

ahead. I continue my pursuit toward the goal, the prize of God's upward calling, in Christ Jesus."
Philippians 3: 13-14

When we feel that our prayers are not being answered, sometimes we experience anxiety, worry, and then, disappointment. There is a divine reasoning that we are not privy to, but we do know that it is always in His Perfect Timing, and His Perfect Plan and Will for our life. So, when doubt starts to creep in our thoughts, we respond,

"I have the strength for everything through Him who empowers me."
Philippians 4: 13

Sometimes the perfect timing has to await a change in us. We are not yet ready to receive his gifts. Pruning and Character Building is important for a strong foundation of faith, trust, and hope. It is then that we experience:

"Then the peace of God that surpasses all understanding will guard your hearts and minds in Christ Jesus."
Philippians 4:7

When we are straining forward, we see with eyes of faith, walking on the water, we trust to follow Him, and know in our hearts that He is strengthening us. Then, peace will reside within you. It goes against everything that we have been conditioned to believe in this world. We have become jaded, tarnished, and that is why Our Merciful Lord is pruning us. Pruning is "to cut off from (a tree or bush) branches, twigs etc. which are diseased or not desired, so as to encourage fruiting or flowering to shape." During this time of discomfort, our prayers should be:

Lord Help Me, I release all things into Your hands and commit myself unto you, trusting you.
Lord Help Me, I ask that You take out of me, add to me or do to me; anything You want.

Character building is to follow the heavenly Christian virtues which combine the classical cardinal virtues and the three theological virtues. It is the ultimate goal of believers in God, in order to be in good moral standing.

Lord Help Me, I Bless You, Praise You, Worship You, and commit all that I am to You, that Your perfect will be done through me.

Lord Help Me, I ask you to make me alert, awake, sharp and attentive in Your thoughts and ways.

Lord Help Me, I ask you to release my warring and ministering angels to minister and war on my behalf.

Lord Help Me, I declare by your power, You are helping and causing me to be bold, dauntless, fearless, confident, intrepid, valiant, steadfast, faithful, true and loyal for Your Name's Sake.

Lord Help Me, I ask for Love and Grace for others and Grace from You Lord. I ask for help that Your Love and Grace in me; flow and be administered to others by Your Spirit in me, to manifest Your Presence in and through me.

Lord Help Me, I ask you to release Your love, joy, peace, patience, kindness, goodness, faithfulness, gentleness, with long-suffering, and self-control to flow over and in and throughout my life. (I ask you to fashion my heart like Yours, that your fruit will abound in and through me to others.)

Lord Help Me, I ask you to help me not be the accuser of the brethren but to teach others in gentleness, to be a help in season, to edify, to exhort and comfort others.

Lord Help Me, I ask that You help me to cease from my own labors. I do so by faith.

Lord Help Me, I ask you to lead me in paths of righteousness for Your Name's Sake.

Lord Help Me, I ask that You cause me to enter Your Rest now, in Jesus' Name and I receive that.

Heavenly Father, I ask that my mind, will and emotions do not deceive me in hearing Your Voice and be still in Jesus' Name.

Heavenly Father, I ask that you shut any doors that need to be shut and open any doors that need to be opened in the spiritual and natural realms in Jesus' Name. I plead the blood of Jesus over those doorways and ask that the enemy be rendered powerless and harmless so they cannot come back through those doorways ever again; to me, my loved ones, family, houses, land, properties, vehicles, work places, schools, and finances in Jesus' Name. Amen!

Prayers From Christian Word Ministries
(www.christianword.org)

We have come full circle, strongholds to be dissolved, brain structure to be altered, mind thoughts controlled, pruning and character building through virtues is our way to freedom. At this present time, we need to be close to God, in order, to be connected to the Truth. We are new creations in Christ Jesus, and He has promised a way in the wilderness. Stop looking behind you, and not before you, the winds are changing and the direction is clear, follow His Way to the Truth, and peace and hope will be restored. He is Our Deliverer and Our Source. He is the Waymaker to our purpose and fulfillment.

THE VOICE OF TRUTH

The Voice of Truth tells me who I am. I am a child of God. I have all the privileges of being His child. I have love, grace, mercy, hope, forgiveness, joy, kindness, protection, compassion, peace and most of all, the truth. I am not perfect, and that is okay. My journey entails striving for perfection. I might never reach it, and that is okay too. What we must do always is to seek the truth. We are told in His Word that the Truth will set us free. Freedom is what we all long for in our lives. So, let us speak the truth.

The truth is that we are all equal and loved by God. God is Our Source of Strength and Hope in a world who seeks to eliminate and separate His existence from our everyday lives.

The world is constantly in flux, but only the Truth remains a constant. The tentacles of evil have reached every nation around the world with its "mantra" that life is not a precious commodity. If life is not precious, then what is? How do we justify our continued lack of interest or care to preserve human life? Where do we go from here? Every life is precious to God and every life is created with a purpose from God. Knowing this, the world has caused an imbalance of sorts for all those sacrificed by due process under the law. It annihilates our divine reason for living in our finite time on this earth. So do we truly believe in our hearts that anything we do here or allow to find its place in our society is of no consequence to our souls? We are spiritual beings placed here in this time to make a difference, and to live our lives in harmony and balance with others, and strive always to obey the laws of the One who created us. In this present time, all believers must follow His Way to the Truth and apply all of His teachings to our lives, so we will survive as spiritual beings.

    Are we so absorbed with self that we can continue down this path of unspeakable and unthinkable actions that the enemy is imposing upon our world? There is no discussion among the masses of these extreme measures taking place in our country, and in the world. Only to the credit of some who rise up as their voices cry out for justice and compassion, only to be quelled with the rhetoric of -isms from the media to silence them against such atrocities. It is no wonder why their agenda just slips past us and becomes part of our "norms". We have only to look upon the younger generations that are rearing their ugly heads in contempt, spewing their hateful rhetoric, desensitized of compassion and void of any human decency in their revolt as a failure. But we still continue to send our children to such institutions and pay them generously for the breaking down of their moral and spiritual foundations. Most parents have spent many years building their child's foundation in love and encouragement for their well-being. In four years or more, academia tears it to pieces, and this is the end result. It is what we are witnessing today on the media, young people void of any humanity.

    This is a world that has been consumed in individualism, whereby; the id and ego are predominant in every decision and circumstance. The id and ego are insatiable in its needs, wants, and desires, therefore, resulting in a lack of empathy for others. That is evil's agenda to tear down and destroy every foundation that we hold sacred. We are watching it enfold on a daily basis. The moral compass doesn't exist anymore, just amoral behavior never before witnessed in this country. So, step by step, we are being acclimated and conditioned to chaos and confusion void of law and order, so that we move forward into destruction and despair. Then, comes the remedy, the solution and the means to end it all, evil's goal. Read history, this has been repeatedly done before. This is what took place in Germany and Russia, a mass brainwashing of a whole society, and the end result was totalitarianism. This massive brainwashing was executed by purging the truth, rewriting history, and stifling freedom of speech, thought, movement, and finally, religion. Now, I have some insight, without judgment, about how the German people lived under Nazism, and the Russian people lived under communism. Two sources permitted this evil shift from a free society to a dictatorship, it was a powerful media, and the apathy of the people.

So why aren't the alarms going off, because the media is your enemy. Their goal is to plunge you into the deepest hole of darkness, as you lie in fear and ignorance. But yet, we continue on believing, accepting and living in this immoral society. Wrong became right, bad became good, lies became truth, and what we are left with is nothingness, emptiness, and a deep despair. This is what the enemy's plan are to seed the fallow land, which is the minds and hearts of our children and future generations.

History that should be noted for its significance. In 1920, Russia was the first country to legalize abortion. In the 1930's, Margaret Sanger, the Birth Control Activist, called the Soviet Union "the country of the liberated woman" during her visit. Her goal, as an activist, clearly stated in such a label, and her obtuse objectives for the future of women, which are illustrated in her associations with vile groups. Yet, she is accredited with the most prominent, courageous pioneer women in history, and many women have proudly accepted awards with her name on it. History does need to be reviewed by all women for the truth.

Truth is that almost all of the women in history who fought for women's rights were opposed to abortion. Perhaps, Susan B. Anthony's statement that "Failure is impossible" underestimated those opposed to women's rights and overestimated our ability to fight for women and children against victimhood. The torch for freedom has a flickering light still left, if we finally reassert our claim for the rights of all persons and become a civilized society with a moral foundation.

Pope Benedict XVI states, "Atheism's cousin is moral relativism – the idea that good and evil are whatever one makes them to be based on one's feeling, the majority consensus on <u>political correctness.</u> It's the pinnacle of individualism whereby all that's left as "the ultimate measure" is only one's ego and desires."

This is the state of this world right now, where life is not held in high regard, and the protection of our children has been abdicated to those whose agenda is to destroy their innocence. Their agenda has infiltrated every level of influence in our society without any protest from us. It is no wonder that the youth is lost and confused in this present time. In <u>1984</u>, Orwell states that "the masses never revolt of their own accord and they never revolt merely because they are oppressed. Discontent can never become articulate." He also states that "robbed of the ability to learn from history and the worries of the future, the Proles (members of the working class) exist in a state of constant present and are incapable of revolution."

"as we look not to what is seen but to what is unseen, for what is seen is transitory, but what is unseen is eternal."
2 Corinthians 4: 18

"for we walk by faith, not by sight"
2 Corinthians 5: 7

"whenever a person turns to the Lord the veil is removed. Now the Lord is the Spirit, and where the Spirit of the Lord is, there is freedom. All of us, gazing with unveiled face on the glory of the Lord, are being transformed into the same image from glory to glory, as from the Lord who is the Spirit."
2 Corinthians 2: 16-18

TIME

Time has seemed to quicken its pace. Each day we move through our routine, without a thought, subjugating our right to free thinking. Our answer is always that we do not have the time to think about any one given subject except our routine. Too much to do, and not enough time seems to be our mantra each day. But is that really true, don't we find time for certain distractions, or have those distractions become part of our routine.

We, as a people, must become aware of the use of our time. Time will pass anyway whether we choose to use it wisely or not. That is why discipline is so imperative when deciding to use your time appropriately. It is important to write it down, goals for the day, week, month or year, make a list of what you want to accomplish in a given time. List it according to priority and refer to it when you wake up in the morning. But first, you must pray. Your time is of value, so make it count, feel satisfied at the end of your day. Start your day with Words from Scripture, "This is the day the Lord has made, let us rejoice and be glad in it." Be thankful and feel blessed in what you have been given and know that this day will never come back again, so make it count.

We live our days consumed with media, from every source, it becomes a roller coaster of emotions that cast its shadow on the future, and all connection to our present day. Once we are saturated with information, there isn't a thought to our immediate goals. Their aim is to occupy the space in your minds, with their agenda.

The media and high tech are seeking to control our time. We must be in control of our time. It has become an addiction, one that we need to break away from in our lives. We are the only ones that can give them the power to influence us, and control our mind thoughts. There was a time when all this technology didn't exist. For those of us who can remember, it was a time of filling our days with leisure of reading, meditating, walking, thinking, spending time with our children, and conversing with others. In this present time, they are encouraging distance from everyone, and shielding our mouths from expressing ourselves, or even to convey a smile. All these rules for a virus that has a 99.5% recovery rate for those under the age of 69. They have found the weapon to be used against us, fear, by the constant barrage of the dangers of this epidemic, only if it's against their agenda. So, this virus is selective, and they seem to know its rules on when and how it transmits. How easily we caved in, and listened to their commands, history will not be kind to us. The religious leaders should be ashamed that there was no push back on closing places of worship. People needed to be closer to God at that time, and those leaders should have complied with God's law, not the law of the city or state. We yielded our rights in panic to the pandemic and continue onward to the path of conformity. It is written in the Bible to never fear, God is always with you.

"For I, the Lord your God, hold your right hand; it is I who say to you, "Fear not, I am the one who helps you."
   Isaiah 41:13

"Peace I leave with you; my peace I give to you. Not as the world gives do I give to you. Let not your hearts be troubled, neither let them be afraid."
Luke 14:27

"You who dwell in the shelter of the Most High, who abide in the shadow of the Almighty, Say to the Lord, "My refuge and my fortress, my God in whom I trust.
For He will rescue you from the snare of the fowler, from the destroying pestilence.
With his pinions he will cover you, and under his wings you shall take refuge; his faithfulness is a buckler and shield. You shall not fear the terror of the night, nor the arrow that flies by day, Not the pestilence that roams in darkness nor the devastating plague at noon. Though a thousand fall at your side, ten thousand at your right side, near you it shall not come."
Psalm 91: 1-7

So where do we place our faith, and trust, it is on Our Savior Jesus Christ, not on earthly direction and guidance. Most of our leaders will fail us, but He will never fail us. We were created for such a time as this, we were fashioned and taught that the Door of Mercy would be open for a time, and then, it would close, and the Door of Justice would then open. I place my hope in Him that by our prayers and petitions He would extend His Mercy. In whatever direction the wind blows, Jesus Christ is Victorious. We must claim His Victory and fight in our full armor, as soldiers of Christ Jesus, and do not become weary. We must never move away from the truth. Do not be swayed by popular opinion and enter into the procession of conformity. Do not fear repercussions, because the alternative of living with their lies is far worse. If you truly know Him, as Savior of the World, The Light of the World, The Risen Christ, Emanuel, Adonai Jehovah, Our Redeemer, Our Restorer, Our Fortress, Our Deliverer, Faithful and True, the Father of Mercies, The Great I Am, you will not falter, but rise as one of His children. Our belief is that our home is in heaven, and we journey this earth in the hope of living eternity with Him. So, fight the good fight, and earn your place in eternal peace. That is our mission and the reason many of us are here in this time. It isn't an accident, there are no accidents with God. We are here with a purpose, live a life worth living, so when your time comes to leave, you will feel fulfillment when you hear "Job Well Done, My loving servant."

SPIRITUAL WARFARE

This world has now entered a different level of warfare on a spiritual level. The stakes are extremely high, in order that the evil agenda can take over this world. So, evil has intensified the flames in their battles for your soul. Much has been written about spiritual warfare, and I also have written a book called On The Frontlines. This book provides a "thought provoking study of human nature." It also "illustrates the relentless, untiring, and ruthless tactics and strategies used against mankind." It is "represented in the "assumed dialogue" of our adversary, evil, while, simultaneously, providing an understanding on how we will rise above our human nature through the Word of God." The book, a masterpiece satire by C. S. Lewis, The Screwtape Letters was the "springboard" of inspiration toward the writing of such a book. In the first line of his book, he states in the preface, "I have no intention of explaining how the correspondence which I now offer to the public fell into my hands." And in the second paragraph, it is important to note as well, "There are two equal and opposite errors into which our race can fall about the devils. One is to disbelieve in their existence. The other is to believe, and to feel an excessive and unhealthy interest in them. They themselves are equally pleased by both errors…." You must know and be aware that evil exist, and our human nature is always at war with our free will to choose good or evil, but our main focus should always be on Our Creator, and the Word of God. For every battle that we encounter, His Word provides the weapons needed to combat the forces against us. Our attire should be His armor of protection; helmet of salvation, breastplate of righteousness, the girdle of truth, the sandals of peace, the shield of faith, the double-edged sword (His Word) and the bow of brass, with the burning arrows to shoot back at the enemy. This attire should be placed on you every day. His Word will equip us for every tactic hurled against us. So, use it proficiently, as we battle this evil that has now pervaded this earth. The evil one's tactics and strategies are now extensive and massive as they pervade the world with its agenda, BUT God is on our side. As I have mentioned in the previous chapter, time is running out. No longer can you sit on the sidelines wishing and hoping that all will be okay. Rather, you must reach for the Word of God and combat as Our Commander-In-Chief, God Almighty, Creator of Heaven and Earth, has commanded through prayer.

Prayer is our most powerful weapon, and as many of you are aware, the enemy does everything to keep us away from prayer. Why? It is simple because that is how it can be defeated. Let God Be God, and He instructs us through His Word to call upon Him for help, protection, guidance and assistance in times of need. A prayer by Christian Word Ministries (2011):

Call On Me

Heavenly Father, I come to you in Jesus Christ's Holy Name. I surrender myself to You, Heavenly Father, Son, and Holy Spirit.

Your Word says in Jeremiah 33 verse 3 to call upon You and You will show me great and mighty things that I do not know. Lord God I come to You and cry out, I surrender all to You. I call unto You, God Creator of Heaven and Earth, I ask You to show me great and mighty things, of the unfathomable riches of Your glory and splendor, all that You are, help me and cause me to plumb the depth of Your Being and know you, I worship You, I praise Your Holy Name, Blessed be your Holy Name. Amen.

In this current climate, the United States, our nation is being tested, and on the verge of a new normal. A new normal based on an ideology to quell our freedoms. What is important at this time is to know your enemy. Your enemy is in the shadows, pulling the strings of all those who claim to know better than you what is the right course for your health, economy, government, and laws. In other words, total control over all of your freedoms and liberty. I ask you at this time to be aware of the tactics and strategies of the enemy to destroy this nation under God, thus planned many centuries ago. When one executes a plan of control over anyone or all subjects, it must first offend their senses to a degree of absurdity and horror. It causes the mind to be in a constant state of fear and trepidation. This disables any thought of resistance, and a clear path for their victory. Our senses are offended on a daily basis by the media as a key tool for their agenda. This path has been studied and exercised in demonstrations around the world to fulfill their need to understand the complexities of human nature. Through great effort, they believe that they have succeeded in their study. In Orwell's book, <u>1984,</u> in his description of Ignorance is Strength, he states how the ruling group can fall from power in four ways. "Either it is conquered from without, or it governs so inefficiently that the masses are stirred to revolt, or it allows a strong and discontented Middle Group to come into being, or it loses its own self-confidence and willingness to govern. These causes do not operate singly, and as a rule all four of them are present in some degree. A ruling class which could guard against all of them would remain in power permanently. Ultimately, the determining factor is the mental attitude of the ruling class itself." (pg. 207)

The enemy is resilient in his plan to destroy all goodness and virtues from this world. The first strategy of the enemy is for:

domi-nation – the exercise of control or influence over someone or something or the state of being controlled. The enemy has cast a worldwide **web** over all countries and has used every form of media communication to fulfill their goal toward domination. They blatantly cheat and lie, withhold information, censor opposing thoughts and words, shame and ridicule any freedom of thought and words. Wolves attempting to herd their sheep toward their direction of control. Those in the shadows of darkness has been conjured up by the evil one to destroy all essence of goodness and justice. If you follow the path of their wealth, you will find that their scheming plots were involved in other countries. That brings me to the enemy's next tactic:

machi-nation – a plot or scheme. Evil waits in the darkness for the precise time to hail their fury on this world. It arrived in the pandemic, given by China, wrapped up in its advantageous means to control the people in this world with fear. These forces are driven by greed and an insatiable desire for power. Our prayers must be our source of strength to overcome machination, and its plan to destroy this world. It has a name, use it in prayer, and ask God to bring it into the light of His Graces. This is a time to use the Sword of the Spirit, The Word of God, to battle this evil, and more important to remember and know who you are, a child of the Most High God.

"Behold, I send you out as sheep in the midst of wolves, so be wise as serpents and innocent as doves."
   Matthew 10: 16

"You belong to God, children, and you have conquered them, for the one who is in you is greater than the one who is in the world. They belong to the world;

accordingly, their teaching belongs to the world, and the world listens to them. We belong to God, and anyone who knows God listens to us, while anyone who does not belong to God refuses to hear us. This is how we know the spirit of truth and the spirit of deceit."
1 John 4: 4-6

"No weapon fashioned against you shall prevail; every tongue you shall prove false that launches an accusation against you. This is the lot of the servants of the Lord, their vindication from me, says the Lord."
Isaiah 54: 17

"Let no one deceive you with empty arguments, for because of these things the wrath of God is coming upon the disobedient. So, do not be associated with them. For you were once darkness, but now you are the light in the Lord. Live as children of light, for light produces every kind of goodness and righteousness and truth."
Ephesians 5: 6-9

"Finally, draw your strength from the Lord and from His mighty power. Put on the armor of God so that you may be able to stand firm against tactics of the devil. For our struggle is not with flesh and blood but with the principalities, with the powers, with the world rulers of this present darkness, with the evil spirits in the heavens."
Ephesians 6: 10-12

"The Lord says to you, 'Do not fear or lose heart at the sight of this vast multitude, for the battle is not yours but God's."
2 Chronicles 20: 15

"For nothing will be impossible for God."
Luke 1: 37

"Amen, I say to you, whatever you bind on earth shall be bound in heaven, and whatever you loose on earth shall be loosed in heaven. Again, Amen, I say to you, if two of you agree on earth about anything for which they are to pray, it shall be granted to them by My Heavenly Father."
Matthew 18: 18-19

In the New American Bible, (1987), Scripture states in the headings in Matthew, Chapter 10:

Coming Persecutions:
"You will be hated by all because of My Name, but whoever endures to the end will be saved."
Matthew 10: 22

Courage under Persecution:
"Therefore, do not be afraid of them. Nothing is concealed that will not be revealed, nor secret that will not be known. What I say to you in the darkness, speak in the light; what you hear whispered, proclaim on the housetops. And do not be afraid of those who kill the body but cannot kill the soul; rather, be afraid of the one who can destroy both soul and body in Gehenna (hell). ...Everyone who acknowledges me before others I will acknowledge before my heavenly Father. But whoever denies me

before others, I will deny before my heavenly Father."
Matthew 10: 26-28, 32-33

And Scripture continues to guide us in the next writing in the Bible, the heading, **Jesus: A Cause of Division.**

"Do not think that I have come to bring peace upon the earth. I have come to bring not peace but the sword."
Matthew 10: 34

Rewards: "Whoever receives you receives me, and whoever receives me receives the one who sent me."
Matthew 10: 40

It is in Isaiah Chapter 40 that we are given by outcome of such evil against us in the heading:

Power of the Creator to Save His People

"Do you not know, or have you not heard? The Lord is the eternal God, creator of the ends of the earth. He does not faint nor grow weary, and his knowledge is beyond scrutiny. He gives strength to the fainting; for the weak he makes vigor abound. Though young men faint and grow weary, and youths stagger and fall. They that hope in the Lord will renew their strength, they will soar as with eagles' wings; They will run and not grow weary, walk and not grow faint."
    Isaiah 40: 28-31

"Fear not, I am with you; be not dismayed, I am your God. I will strengthen you, and help you, and uphold you with my right hand of justice."
    Isaiah 41: 10

By faith we who know Him, know that we are never alone in this battle. "He is The Waymaker, Miracle Worker, Promise Keeper, and the Light in the Darkness, My God that is who you are." (Song - The Waymaker, Leeland). "Make way through the waters, walk me through the fire, do what you are famous for, shut the mouths of lions, bring dry bones to life, do what you are famous for, I believe in you," (Song by Tauren Wells – Famous For (I Believe). He has given us His Word, and we can and shall use His Word as a double-edged sword (having two cutting edges), and the assistance of the angels, which I will cover in the next chapter. I will continue with the tactics and strategies in this current warfare of evil against goodness and justice. When one is in battle, it is important to gain knowledge and understanding of the adversary, in order, to know the enemy. So, I will define the difference between tactics and strategies. Tactics are <u>short</u> term, "an action or method that is planned and used to achieve **a particular goal**."

Strategies are <u>long</u> term, "a plan of action or policy designed to achieve **a major or overall aim.**"

The evil tactics of machi**nation** used by the enemy through the strategy of domi**nation** for the sole purpose of his plan for dam**nation** (condemnation to eternal punishment in hell) are:

Indig**nation** – anger or annoyance provoked by what is perceived as unfair treatment.

Profa**nation** – not respectful of orthodox religious practice, irreverent, obscene, blasphemous.

Fulmi**nation** – an expression of vehement protest.

Abomi**nation** – a feeling hatred, a thing that causes disgust or hatred.

Subor**nation** – bribe or otherwise induce (someone) to commit an unlawful act.

Subornare "incite secretly"

Condem**nation** – the expression of very strong disapproval; censure.

Rui**nation** – the state of being ruined.

Supi**nation** – the act of lying.

Indoctri**nation** – the process of teaching a person or group to accept a set of beliefs uncritically.

Recrimi**nation** – an accusation brought by the accused against the accuser upon the same fact.

Expug**nation** – conquest, the act of taking by assault.

Divi**nation** – the practice of seeking knowledge of the future or the unknown by supernatural means.

Vacci**nation** – inoculation, treatment with a vaccine to produce immunity against a disease.

Alie**nation** – the state or experience of being isolated from a group or an activity to which one should belong, or in which one should be involved.

    Today, in these times, evil is blatant in the use of these tactics and strategies to gain total power over this world. All of these tactics will result in tearing down the spirit of individuals, so they become pliable to the demands and commands of those who desire to be in power. I repeat, all of these tactics have been infiltrated in countries as a strategy in the past, review history while you still have access to information.

HEAVENLY ASSISTANCE ANGELS

Who are angels? The definition in the dictionary is "a spiritual being believed to act as an attendant, agent, or messenger of God, conventionally represented in human form with wings and a long robe. (American Dictionary of the English Language)

Angels are arranged in groups called "choirs", there are nine choirs of angels. The Highest are the Seraphim, Cherubim, Thrones, associated with love, knowledge and power. In the middle are Dominions, Powers, Virtues, which functions with the universal governance of creation. And the lower hierarchy are Principalities, Archangels, and Angels are concerned with direct administration of creatures in the world. These are arranged and split in triads, (a group or set of three connected people or things). All of these choirs should be called upon in the Name of God for assistance, protection, direction, and guidance, and one must never forget that each of us has been assigned a guardian angel for life. It is important at this time to call upon these angels to assist us in health, protection, and guidance every day and thank them each time for coming to our assistance. We are only separated by time and space. So, ask for Heavenly assistance in all your endeavors to assure and insure the proper and most timely expediency of your prayers to God.

Chaplet of The Angels
Act of Contrition
O God come to my assistance.
O Lord make haste to help me.
Glory Be....

Nine Salutations, each in honor of each choir of Angels, after salutation say one Our Father, and three Hail Mary.

First Salutation – By the intercession of St. Michael and the heavenly choir of Seraphim, may it please God to make us

worthy to receive into our hearts the fire of His perfect charity. Amen.

Second Salutation – By the intercession of St. Michael and the heavenly choir of Cherubim, may God in His good pleasure, grant us grace to abandon the ways of sin, and follow the path of Christian perfection. Amen

Third Salutation – By the intercession of St. Michael and the heavenly choir of Thrones, may it please God to infuse into our hearts the spirit of true and sincere humility. Amen

Fourth Salutation – By the Intercession of St. Michael and the heavenly choir of Dominations, may it please God to grant us peace to have dominion over our senses, and to correct our depraved passions. Amen

Fifth Salutation – By the intercession of St. Michael and the heavenly choir of the Powers, may God vouchsafe to keep our souls from the wiles and temptations of the devil. Amen

Sixth Salutation – By the intercession of St. Michael and the Admiral Heavenly Virtues, may it please God to keep us from falling into temptation, and may He deliver us from evil. Amen

Seventh Salutation – By the intercession of St. Michael and the heavenly choir of Principalities, may it please God to fill our souls with the spirit of true and sincere obedience. Amen

Eighth Salutation – By the intercession of St. Michael and the heavenly choir of Archangels, may it please God to grant the gift of perseverance in the faith and in all good works, that we may be thereby enabled to attain the glory of paradise. Amen

Ninth Salutation – By the intercession of St. Michael and the heavenly choir of all angels, may God vouchsafe to grant us their guardianship through this mortal life, and after death a happy entrance into the everlasting glory of heaven. Amen

Four Our Fathers – St. Michael, St. Gabriel, St. Raphael, and our Guardian Angel.

Anthem and Prayer

O Glorious Prince St Michael the Archangel, chief and commander of the Heavenly Hosts, guardian of souls, vanquisher of rebel spirits, steward of the palace of God under Jesus Christ and our admirable conductor, thou who dost shine with excellence and virtues; vouchsafe to deliver us from every evil; who with full confidence have recourse to Thee; and enable us by thy gracious protection to serve God more and more faithfully every day.

\V. Pray for us, most blessed Michael, Prince of the Church of Jesus Christ.

R. That we may be made worthy of His promises.

The following prayer is one of the most powerful prayers that should be recited every day to St. Michael, The Archangel, the Powerful Intercessor. It was introduced by Pope Leo XIII on October 13, 1884, after a Mass where he was led to his chambers to write this prayer. The story of the origins of this prayer is that Pope Leo XIII heard a conversation between God and Satan. Satan asked for more time and power to destroy God's church for 75 to 100 years, and God granted him his request. In return, God gave Pope Leo this prayer to be said at every Mass after the Eucharist celebration and this was done for sixty years. Then, Pope Paul VI put an end to it, after the Second Vatican Council. By the Grace of God on April 24, 1994 in St. Peter's Square, Pope John Paul II restored this powerful prayer and encouraged people to recite it against the forces of evil. In the New Testament, Revelations, St. Michael's role is one of protector and the leader of the army of God against the forces of evil, and to assist the dying at the hour of their death.

"Then the war broke out in heaven, Michael and his angels battled against the dragon. The dragon and its angels fought back; but they did not prevail and there was no longer any place for them in heaven. The huge dragon, the ancient serpent, who is called the Devil and Satan, who deceived the whole world was thrown down to earth, and its angels were thrown down with it."
Revelations 12: 7-9

....."Therefore, rejoice, you heavens, and you who dwell in them. But woe to you, earth and sea, for the Devil has come down to you in great fury, for he knows he has but a short time."
Revelations 12:1

Prayer To St. Michael The Archangel

Saint Michael the Archangel, defend us in battle, be our protection against the wickedness and snares of the devil. May God rebuke him, we humbly pray, and do thou, O Prince of the Heavenly Host, by the power of God, thrust into hell Satan and all the evil spirits who prowl about the world seeking the ruin of souls. Amen.

In the name of the Father, and of the Son, and of the Holy Spirit. Amen

Prayer for those who are dying:

Almighty and Eternal God, who in Thine own marvelous goodness and pity didst, for the common salvation of man, choose the glorious Archangel Michael to be the prince of the Church; make us worthy, we pray Thee, to be delivered by his beneficent protection from all our enemies, that, at the hour of our death, none of them may approach to harm us; do thou vouchsafe unto us that by the same Archangel Michael, we may be introduced into the presence of Thy most high and divine majesty, through the merits of the same Jesus Christ Our Lord. Amen

This Unity Prayer was given to a woman, Elizabeth Kindelmann who receives messages from Jesus Christ. It is a powerful prayer that I wish to share, it is said that it will blind Satan, and souls will not be led into sin. Prayer is a powerful weapon in your hands.

<u>Unity Prayer</u>

May Our Feet journey together, May Our Hands gather in unity, May Our Hearts beat in unison, May Our Souls be in harmony, May Our Thoughts be as one, May Our Ears listen to the silence together, May Our Glances profoundly penetrate each other, May Our Lips pray together to gain mercy from the Eternal Father. Amen.

I have allowed all of these prayers to become a part of my book, because they are powerful weapons in battle. So, use the weapons that Jesus has placed into your hands to insure your victory in His Name.

FOLLOW THE LIGHT

"God is the truth. There is only one True Truth. "God's Word reveals to us that He Is Light (truth) and in Him there is no darkness (lies and deception).

"No one has ever seen God. The only Son, God, who is at the Father's side, has revealed Him."
John 1: 18

"In the beginning was the Word, and the Word was with God, and the Word was God. He was in the beginning with God. All things came to be through him, and without him nothing came to be. What came to be through him was life, and this life was the light of the human race; the light shines in the darkness, and the darkness has not overcome it."
John 1: 1-5

"But you are a chosen race, a royal priesthood, a holy nation, a people of His own, so that you may announce the praises of Him who called you out of darkness into His wonderful light."
1 Peter 2: 9

"Your Word is a lamp to my feet and a light to my path."
Psalm 119: 105

"You are a light of the world. A city set on a hill cannot be hidden."
Matthew 5: 14

"I have come into the world as light, so that whoever believes in me may not remain in darkness."
John 12: 46

The definition of light as referred to in these Scriptures, is "understanding, insight, enlightenment, illumination, awareness, comprehension, edification, clarification, explanation, knowledge. One antonym in the dictionary is ignorance. Phrases pertaining to light are "bring something to light" which is to "reveal, unveil, manifest and to "see the light" is to "understand, get the message." "True Revelation can only come to those who have a relationship with God through Jesus Christ. The Truth will not only reveal new aspects about God, but He will also open up new insights, wisdom, and revelations about life, self, and others around you and the way you perceive the world. Things will change because the touch of the Creator changes all who choose Him." (Christian Ministries pg. viii) Jesus Christ is the Light of the World. His light manifests in love and illuminates our conscience to do what is right. He enlightens us to the path that we should take in our journey on earth. His Word provides an explanation and a clarification to true knowledge as we comprehend our place and purpose in this world. His Way is the only way to truth. So, we have come full circle. The truth is what our quest should be at all times of our lives. We must always seek the truth in life or die in ignorance.

"What fellowship does light have with darkness? …Therefore, do not associate with them, for once you were darkness, but now you are light in the Lord…Take no part in the unfruitful works of darkness, but instead expose them."
2 Corinthians 6: 14, Ephesians 5: 7-11

This present time is not for the weak of heart or for those who wish to remain lukewarm or to sit on the fence. This is a time for choosing your side whether to walk by faith in truth or shuffle your feet by conformity in lies, the light or darkness, your choice. But you must make a choice.

"And this is the verdict, that the light came into the world, but people preferred darkness to light, because their works were evil. For everyone who does wicked things hates the light and does not come toward the light, so that his works might not be exposed. But whoever lives the truth comes to the light, so that his works may be clearly seen as done in God."
John 3: 19-21

Our conscience always reveals to us what is right and wrong. We can falter at times, but if we are aware of the wrong that we are doing, or saying, then, we have made our choice. And if we repeatedly make the wrong choice, then we are lost. Jesus Christ came to this world, so we can have peace and a worthy life. His life is an example of how we achieve this goal. His Word provides a guideline to live a Christian life. When the time comes that Our Lord, and Savior Jesus Christ returns, let us be worthy to share eternal salvation in heaven with Him. The time draws near, you must make a choice.

"But of that day and hour no one knows, not even the angels of heaven, nor the Son, but the Father alone."
Matthew 24:36

OUR MOTHER IN HEAVEN

The Mother of God, the Patroness of the United States of America, the Queen of Peace, and most important, the Co – Redemptrix of all of us, we pray to her for freedom and peace, and to guide us upon our path back home to Her Son Jesus Christ. The Blessed Mother has many titles and has appeared in many countries to warn us against the evil one. She has been very active in the last century, and in the present time, to warn us that we must become closer to God and pray the rosary. The rosary is a weapon; it is an armor against evil. Prayer is life to our soul, and the rosary helps us to meditate on the mysteries of the lives of Jesus and Mary. Our Lady of the Rosary is our intercessor to strengthen our hearts and souls to follow Christ. Many spiritual battles have been won by saying the rosary. An exorcist said that he heard the devil say during an exorcism: Every Hail Mary is like a blow on my head. If Christians knew how powerful the Rosary was, it would be my end.

"At the foot of the cross there begins the entrusting of humanity to the Mother of Christ....   Pope John Paul II

For women, the Blessed Mother is a symbol of strength, and courage in our faith. She epitomizes the ideals and virtues of a perfect woman. She annihilates the ego and desires of our human nature. Eve succumbed to human nature, and the compelling forces of individualism, which is form and content in a lesser nature than what God created us to be. Eve chose ego and a trust in her own instincts; Our Blessed Mother chose faith and a trust in God.

We, as women, are driven by our past fears, in order, to control circumstances or situations in life. Fear will always lead us in the wrong direction. The road is slippery when trying to embark on a road with illusive control. Women are moving away from faith in a Supreme Being, and towards the slippery slope of individualism. Without faith, we remain victims of the destiny being fulfilled by others to create the "damsel in distress." We place our "head in the sand" and that term is defined as "to refuse to think about unpleasant facts although they will have an influence on your situation." Like Eve, we have succumbed to the deception of rationalization to justify our actions, behavior, and attitude, even if, it is not appropriate and in alignment to our moral values.

Our Blessed Mother represents the highest hierarchy of women, the Refuge Of Our Times. Jesus said to Elizabeth Kindelmann, The Flame of Love, pg. 109, **"My Mother is Noah's Ark."** We must *invite* Our Blessed Mother to accompany us in *everything* we do. Jesus pronounced to John **"Behold your mother."**

"And from that hour the disciple took her into his home."
John 19: 27

It is in this present time that we must ask for her help and assistance, and invite Her into our homes. Time is running out, and we are heading over the cliff. We have lost our connection to the truth. Women have lost empathy for each other because we have been divided by rhetoric. In the streets, you hear women ranting in protest for their rights, but those that lead are not interested in your rights. Those in charge are feeding you rhetoric and lies for huge corporations, elite power, and hungry agendas. They are leading you into darkness. Time to wake up, and evaluate your position in society, while seeking the truth for laws that pertain to the welfare of all women. We are women, not men. We lost our strength, when we gave up who we are in exchange for lies.

The best example for all women to follow is Our Blessed Mother. The Blessed Mother lived a virtuous life, and an example of faith, courage, strength, and love for all people. In all of the apparitions around the world, She pleads for all of us to come closer to Her Son Jesus Christ, and to pray the rosary. This has been her message for more than a century. If we follow Her directions, the truth will give you the freedom that women have desired for many centuries. We deserve better than what we have received. Wake Up from your sleep, and realize what is occurring in this present time.

Complacency (Sleepwalking)

"In sleep, we have closed off any means of communication to the truth. We have lost all awareness of our present circumstances. We are dreamers in a dream who have bought into the illusion of the world's concepts and ideals. By our desire to remain asleep, we have become lulled by their measure of acceptability. It is no wonder at this time why everything seems to escape our notice. Every idea rises in triumph upon the pressures to carry on this façade of indifference. We have become sleepwalkers, who have been veiled by the web of deception. This web entangles our thoughts and wraps our hearts in solitude, and finally destroys the essence of any connection of truth to our self-worth." (Louise Scarmato)

The Wings of Dawn, pg. 19

In the Merriam-Webster Dictionary, womanhood is defined as "the condition of being a woman, the qualities considered to be natural to or characteristic of a woman." In the past, this term was properly defined within the core of every woman against the backlash of injustice and inequality. Women identified in those times with their constant struggle against the laws of society. In this present time, women became complacent by willingly accepting the role granted to them by society. In this time and space, society has riveted us to a "spot" with a distorted meaning to who we are, and this is causing a "standoff" among us. This "standoff" disallows women of opposing positions to converge in the pursuit of a solution to our current problems. Without our input, society is allowed to integrate laws and standards that they deem acceptable for women. Therefore, resurrecting the same theme of resignation and acceptance that we have courageously fought against in the past.

We are enslaved to rhetoric, as we move along in conformity, and treated as victims that need their governance on our lives. What we should be compelled to do is to follow His Way to the truth, which has been ordained in love for our gender since the beginning of time. There lies our road to freedom, which will glorify the true meaning of womanhood.

Let the truth surface in order to reach the higher purpose by which we were created, void of the world's intentions toward us, as women. There wisdom lies, and holds all of the answers and the key to our fulfillment.

"Blessed are you who believed that what was spoken to you by the Lord would be fulfilled."
Luke 1: 45

"For just as woman came from man, so man is born of woman; but all things are from God."
1 Corinthians 11: 12

"God is in the midst of her; she shall not be moved; God will help her when morning dawns."
Psalm 46: 5

"But by the grace of God I am what I am…
1 Corinthians 15: 10

"Strength and dignity are her clothing, and she laughs at the days to come."
Proverbs 31: 25

APPARITIONS, MESSAGES AND PRAYERS

Our Blessed Mother has been appearing to people all over the world for the past century. These appearances are called Marian Apparitions. An apparition is "a supernatural appearance of a person, an unusual or unexpected sight, the act of appearing or being visible." Marian Apparitions is the appearance of Our Blessed Mother who is coming from heaven to earth to convey messages of profound importance, which concern our faith and the coming events in this world. The Blessed Mother is our mantle of protection. Her appearances have been noted all over the world. She appears to a seer, who is a person that can faithfully and accurately relay Her message with God's grace. The nature of the visit to a seer can be one short appearance to several over the course of years. Approved Apparitions must have "sincerity and habitual docility towards Ecclesiastical Authority." The Vatican and bishops must confirm that there is nothing contradictory to the Faith in the messages that have emerged from the apparitions, visions are credible, and that the Virgin Mary can be venerated under that specific title attributed to her. Just to name a few: Our Lady of Guadalupe (1531), Our Lady Undoer of the Knots (1700) Our Lady of LaSalette (1846), Our Lady of Lourdes (1858), Our Lady of Beauraing (1932), Our Lady of Knock (1879), Our Lady of Fatima (1917),

Queen of Peace, Mother of the Redeemer, (Medjugorje (between mountains), 1981).

On May 12, 2019, Pope Francis authorized pilgrimages to Medjugorje considering the "considerable flow of people who go to Medjugorje and the abundant fruits of grace that have sprung from it." Pope John Paul II speaks of Our Lady of Fatima's intercession regarding the event of 5/13/1981 when he was in mortal danger. He says, "By Her intercession, his life was given back to him."

Mary Immaculate, Patroness of the United States of America

**O God our Creator,
From your provident hand we have received our right to life, liberty, and the pursuit of happiness. You have called us as your people and given us the right and the duty to worship you, the only true God, and your Son, Jesus Christ.
Through the power and working of your Holy Spirit, you call us to live out our faith in the midst of the world, bringing the light**

and the saving truth of the Gospel to every corner of society.

We ask you to bless us in our vigilance for the gift of religious liberty. Give us the strength of mind and heart to readily defend our freedoms when they are threatened; give us courage in making our voices heard on behalf of the rights of your Church and the freedom of conscience of all people of faith.

Grant, we pray, O heavenly Father, a clear and united voice to all your sons and daughters gathered in your Church in this decisive hour in the history of our nation, so that, with every trial withstood and every danger overcome – for the sake of our children, our grandchildren, and all who come after us – this great land will always be "one nation, under God, indivisible, with liberty and justice for all."

We ask this through Christ Our Lord. Amen.

(by DeSales Media Group, Inc. FORTNIGHT FOR FREEDOM).

Our Blessed Mother began appearing to six young people in Yugoslavia, in a small village called Medjugorje since June 24, 1981. At first, there were daily messages, then in 1984, Our Lady told them the messages would be weekly every Thursday, in 1987, then, She told them on the 25th of each month that her messages were for the salvation of the world and to lead the world back to Her Son. These monthly messages are still continuing today.

Here are the messages of Our Lady, Queen of Peace, from December 25, 2019 - March 25, 2021.

December 25, 2019
Our Lady appeared to Jakov Coloi at 2:25 p.m. and the apparition lasted 9 minutes. Our Lady came with Little Jesus in Her arms.
(Before Pandemic)
"Dear children, today, on this day of grace, in a special way I am calling you to open your hearts and to implore Jesus to strengthen your faith. Children, through prayer with the heart, faith and works, you will come to know what is means to live a

sincere Christian life. Often times, children, darkness, pain and crosses overwhelm your hearts. Do not waver in faith and ask "why" because you think that you are alone and abandoned. Instead, open your hearts, pray and believe firmly and then your heart will feel God's nearness and that God never abandons you – that He is beside you at every moment. Through prayer and faith, God will answer your every "why" and transform your every pain, darkness, and cross into light. Thank you."

Also, another message on that day:

"Dear children! I am carrying my Son Jesus to you, for Him to bless you and reveal to you His love, which comes from Heaven. Your heart yearns for peace, of which there is less and less on earth. That is why people are far from God and souls are sick and heading toward spiritual death. I am with you, little children, to lead you on this way of salvation to which God calls you. Thank you for having responded to my call."

**(Time of Quarantine)
March 25, 2020**

"Dear children! I am with you all these years to lead you to the way of salvation. Return to My Son; return to prayer and fasting. Little children permit for God to speak to your heart, because satan is reigning and wants to destroy your lives and the earth on which you walk. Be courageous and decide for holiness. You will see conversion in your hearts and families; prayer will be heard; God will hear your cries and give you peace. I am with you and am blessing you all with my motherly blessing. Thank you for having responded to my call.

April 25, 2020

"Dear children! May this time be an incentive for personal conversion for you. Pray, little children, in solitude, to the Holy Spirit to strengthen you in faith and trust in God, that you may be worthy witnesses of the love which God bestows upon you through my presence. Little children do not permit trials to harden your heart and for prayer to be like a desert. Be a reflection of God's love and witness the Risen Jesus by your lives. I am with you and I love all of you with my motherly love. Thank you for having responded to my call."

May 25, 2020

"Dear children! Pray with me for a new life for all of you. In your hearts, little children, you know what needs to be changed. Return to God and His Commandments, so that the Holy Spirit may change your lives and the face of this earth, which is in need of renewal in the spirit. Little children, be prayer for all those who do not pray, be joy for all those who do not see the way out; be carriers of light in the darkness of this peaceless time. Pray and seek the help and protection of the saints so that you also could yearn for Heaven and Heavenly realities. I am with you and am protecting and blessing all of you with my motherly blessing. Thank you for having responded to my call."

June 25, 2020

"Dear children! I am listening to your cries and prayers, and am interceding for you before My Son, Jesus, who is the Way, the Truth and the Life. Return, little children, to prayer and open your hearts in this time of grace and set out on the way of conversion. Your life is passing and, without God, does not have meaning. This is why I am with you to lead you towards holiness of life, so that each of you may discover the joy of living. I love you all, little children, and am blessing you with my motherly blessing. Thank you for having responded to my call."

July 25, 2020

"Dear children! In this peaceless time in which the devil is harvesting souls to draw them to himself, I am calling you to persevering prayer, so that in prayer you discover the God of love and hope. Little children take the cross in your hands. May it be your encouragement for love to always win, in a special way now when the cross and faith are rejected. You be a reflection and an example with your lives that faith and hope are still alive, and a new world of peace is possible. I am with you and intercede for you before My Son, Jesus. Thank you for having responded to my call."

August 25, 2020

"Dear children! This is a time of grace. I am with you and anew am calling you, little children: return to God and to prayer until prayer will be a joy for you. Little children, you do not have a future or peace until your life begins with a personal conversion and a change to the good. Evil will cease and peace will begin to reign in your hearts and in the world. Therefore, little children, pray, pray,

pray. I am with you and intercede before My Son, Jesus, for each of you. Thank you for having responded to my call."

September 25, 2020

"Dear children! I am with you for so long because God is great in His love and in my presence. I am calling you, little children: return to God and to prayer. May the measure (way of) living be love and do not forget, little children, that prayer and fasting work miracles in you and around you. May everything you do be for the glory of God, and then Heaven will fill your heart with joy, and you will feel that God loves you and is sending me to save you and the earth on which you live. Thank you for having responded to my call."

October 25, 2020

"Dear children! At this time, I am calling you to return to God and to prayer. Invoke the help of all the saints, for them to be an example and a help to you. satan is strong and is fighting to draw all the more hearts to himself. he wants war and hatred. That is why I am with you for this long, to lead you to the way of salvation, to Him who is the Way, the Truth, and the Life. Little children return to the love for God and He will be your strength and refuge. Thank you for having responded to my call."

November 25, 2020

"Dear children! This is a time of love, warmth, prayer and joy. Pray, little children, for little Jesus to be born in your hearts. Open your hearts to Jesus who gives Himself to each of you. God sent me to be joy and hope in this time, and I am saying to you: Without little Jesus you do not have the tenderness or the feeling of Heaven which is hidden in the Newborn. Therefore, little children, work on yourselves. By reading the Sacred Scriptures, you will discover Jesus' birth and joy, as in the first days which Medjugorje gave to mankind. History will be truth which, also today, is being repeated in you and around you. Work on and build peace through the Sacrament of Confession. Reconcile with God, little children, and you will see miracles around you. Thank you for having responded to my call."

December 25, 2020

"Dear children, also today Jesus is here beside you, even when you think that you are alone, and that light does not exist in your life. He is here and has never left you, or distanced Himself from you. The light of His birth illuminates this world and your life. His Heart is always open towards you to receive your every pain, every trial, fear and need. His arms are extended towards you, that as a father, He may embrace you and tell you how important you are for Him, how much He loves you and cares for His children. Children, is your heart open towards Jesus? Have you completely surrendered your life into His hands? Have you accepted Jesus as your father, to whom you can always turn and in Him find consolation and everything you need to live true faith? That is why, my children, surrender your hearts to Jesus and permit Him to begin to rule your lives because only in this way, will you accept the present and be able to face the world in which you live today. With Jesus, every fear, suffering and pain disappear, because your heart accepts His will and everything that comes into your life. Jesus will give you the faith to accept everything and nothing will distance you from Him – because He firmly holds you by the hand, and does not permit for you to distance and lose yourselves in difficult moments –because He has become the Lord of your life. I bless you with my motherly blessing."

January 25, 2021

"Dear children! I am calling you at this time to prayer, fasting, and renunciation that you may be stronger in faith. This is a time of awakening and of giving birth. As nature which gives itself, you also, little children, ponder how much you have received. Be joyful bearers of peace and love that it may be good for you on earth. Yearn for Heaven; and in Heaven there is no sorrow or hatred. That is why, little children, decide anew for conversion and let holiness begin to reign in your life. Thank you for having responded to my call."

Renunciation – very strict self-denial, the giving up of a claim or right.

February 25, 2021

"Dear children!
God has permitted me to be with you also today, to call you to prayer and fasting. Live this time of grace and be witnesses of hope, because I repeat to you, my children, that with prayer and fasting also wars can be suppressed. Little children, believe and live this time of grace in faith and with faith; and My Immaculate Heart does not leave any of you in peacelessness if you have recourse to me. I intercede for you before

the Most High and I pray for peace in your hearts and for hope for the future. Thank you for having responded to my call."

March 25, 2021
"Dear children! Also today I am with you: Little children, who prays does not fear the future and does not lose hope. You are chosen to carry joy and peace, because you are mine. I have come here with the name "Queen of Peace" because the devil wants peacelessness and war, he wants to fill your heart with fear of the future - but the future is God's. That is why, be humble and pray, and surrender everything into the hands of the Most High who created you, Thank you for having responded to my call."

The messages of the past year convey the love and devotion of Our Blessed Mother and Our Savior Jesus Christ for all of us during this year of the pandemic. I started by only just a few, but after reading them, I felt compelled to write most of them in the succession that they were received by the seer. Each one of them have a profound message to strengthen our faith in these turbulent times. The messages were given by Our Mother for spiritual direction because She loves us. Its importance is unprecedented for these times and one can never be assured of their accessibility due to the censoring and control of high tech. So this book will give you the access to Her messages of love. On Our Lady of Medjugorje Monthly Message for the World, you can find messages from the previous years.

The Blessed Mother is always pointing in the direction toward her Son, Jesus Christ. Just as she said at the Wedding Feast of Cana **"Do whatever he tells you."**

The chapter on Our Blessed Mother has been extensive due to the signs of the times. Elizabeth Kindelmann was given this message, "When you say the prayer that honors Me, The Hail Mary, include this petition:

Hail Mary, full of grace; the Lord is with thee; blessed art thou among women, and blessed is the fruit of thy womb, Jesus. Holy Mary, Mother of God, pray for us sinners,

spread the effect of grace of Thy Flame of Love over all of humanity, now and at the hour of our death. Amen.

I was led to this beautiful prayer to the Blessed Mother to implore her love and protection through the wounds of Our Lord Jesus Christ for the whole world. It was on the back of the Divine Mercy Chaplet pamphlet. I was compelled to share it.

Prayer: Our Mother engulf the whole world with the torch of your love full of grace now and at the hour of our death, Amen. (10x)
Come, Holy Spirit, fill the hearts of your faithful and enkindle in them the fire of your love.
Pray for each wound (One Our Father, Hail Mary, Glory Be) Precious Blood of Jesus save us and the whole world. (10 times)
Wound of right hand
Wound of left hand
Wound right foot of Jesus

Wound left foot of Jesus
Piercing side of Jesus

Prayer: Behold the Cross of the Lord; be scattered ye hostile powers. The Lion of the tribe of Judah, the root of David, has conquered!
Pray: Our Mother save us by thy loving flame of your Immaculate Heart. (10x)

Every home should have holy water, make the sign of the cross and say, **"By this holy water and by Thy Precious Blood wash away my sins O Lord."**

The devil hates holy water because it has power over him.

PLOT TWIST

What is a plot twist? A plot twist introduces a radical change in the direction or expected outcome of the plot. When it happens near the end of a story, it is known as a twist or surprise ending. A plot twist may be foreshadowed to prepare the audience to accept it.

The year 2020 has been a difficult year regarding every aspect of our lives. It is a year where perseverance, fortitude, courage, and faith, hope, and trust in God is stretched to its breaking point. For most of us, who are believers, we pray for mercy and the will to continue on in faith and trust in Our Savior Jesus Christ. He does not abandon us, so we must never lose hope. His love will never fail us.

"Now hope does not disappoint, because the love of God has been poured out in our hearts by the Holy Spirit who was given to us."
Romans 5: 5

Our God is the God of Plot Twist, and it is found throughout the Bible, but I will focus on the greatest one. The ultimate plot twist on this earth was the Resurrection Of Jesus Christ. As Jesus walked the earth to fulfill His Divine Mission, He had many followers. But, in the end during the passion, the disciples believed that His mission had failed. Even though, they were witness to the Last Supper, and miracles, they believed that earthly forces proved more powerful than His Kingdom in Heaven. Through all of the trials and passions of Christ from the Agony in the Garden to the Crucifixion where Our Lord was tortured beyond recognition, his followers were hiding in terror and anguish. They believed it was the end of His Mission, and the ending of the life of the greatest man that ever walked this earth. Three days later, empty tomb, and He rose from the dead, the Resurrection – Plot Twist. The Resurrection brought hope, forgiveness, redemption, proof of His Deity, and the promise of eternal salvation. The foreshadowing is written in John Chapter 14 – Last Supper Discourse:

> **"Do not let your hearts be troubled. You have faith in God, have faith also in me. In my Father's house there are many dwelling places. If there were not, would I have told you that I am going to prepare a place for you? And if I go and prepare a place for you, I will come back again and take you to myself, so that where I am you also may be."**
> **John 14: 1-3**

As believers, it is in this time of unrest, and disbelief about the events happening in the world, we await a plot twist. Our Savior did not abandon us, He would never forsake us. Know your enemy and understand that this plan has been prophesied in Revelations, and the One True God Almighty, Jesus Christ and the leagues of Angels are victorious in the end. The victory is given to us by Our Savior of the World. Plot Twist.

Amongst the corruption, the deceit, and machinations happening, we are in a state that is unbelievable and offensive to our senses. We look for relief and a means to escape or even to ignore the hypocrisy and blatant lies hurled at us on a continuous daily basis. This is such a time when our faith will be tested to an extreme measure of endurance. Again, the winds are blowing and moving us upon an unrecognizable path toward the direction of the unknown. A massive plan to annihilate our way of life and take away our freedoms. It's happening all around us, like a freight train, moving at an excessive speed to halt all thoughts of resistance. It's coming from every angle of offense into our homes, schools, jobs, and government. It's the battle for our time, and a war waged against us insidiously planned by evil to quell all moral, critical and processed thought from your mind and heart. So, what do we do? How do we proceed against such an evil plan? Continue to pray earnestly and deliberately for this country and the world, do not lose faith and believe that God would ever abandon us, He is in control, He is the Great I Am, Emannuel – God with us.

"My grace is sufficient for you, for My strength is made perfect in weakness."
2 Corinthians 12: 9

Before the soldiers came to arrest Jesus, He spoke to His apostles about His departure from this earth into heaven, he instructed them on to how proceed forward without Him.

"Remain in me, as I remain in you. Just as a branch cannot bear fruit on its own unless it remains on the vine, so neither can you unless you remain in me. I am the vine you are the branches. Whoever remains in me, and I in him will bear much fruit, because without me you can do nothing. Anyone who does not remain in me will be thrown out like a branch and wither; people will gather them and throw them into a fire, and they will be burned. If you remain in me and my words remain in you, ask for whatever you want, and it will be done for you."
John 15: 4-7

"If the world hates you, realize that it hated me first. If you belonged to the world, the world would love its own; but because you do not belong to the world, and I have

chosen you out of the world, the world hates you."
    John 15: 18-19

"But I tell you the truth, it is better for you that I go. For if I do not go, the Advocate will not come to you. But if I go, I will send him to you. And when he comes, he will convict the world in regard to sin and righteousness and condemnation: sin, because they do not believe in me; righteousness, because I am going to the Father and you will no longer see me; condemnation, because the ruler of this world has been condemned."
    John 16: 7-11

"I have much more to tell you, but you cannot bear it now. But when he comes, the Spirit of truth, he will guide you to all truth."
    John 16:12-13

"I have told you this so that you might have peace in me. In the world you will have

trouble, but take courage, I have conquered the world."
John 16: 33

"I gave them your word, and the world hated them, because they do not belong to the world any more than I belong to the world. I do not ask that you take them out of the world but that you keep them from the evil one."
John 17: 14-15

The wind is still blowing, constantly in motion, as isolation brings awareness of just who we are. We are being brought down to the bare necessities of life, our heart and soul. Where do you stand? What do you stand for? Will you take a stand? Questions pondered, as our resources diminish, and our cares and worries increase. Yet, deep within our heart and soul we know the source of our strength and hope. It is God who loves us unconditionally. Time to hunker down and pray deliberately for each petition before the Lord. **Revive** – return to consciousness or life, become active or flourishing again; **Restore** – bring back, from a depressed, inactive or unused state; **Renew** – in the mind and memory, **Rekindle** – relight a fire, **Resurrect** – bring back new vigor to life; **Revivify** -give new life; **Refresh** – give new strength and energy, reinvigorate, update knowledge, stimulate someone's memory. Such a time as this calls for the seven R's to be given to us by grace from Our God. These times call for courage in the face of fear and uncertainty, but a courage derived from the grace and mercy of Almighty God. During times of isolation, we become more aware of the condition of our souls. Are we ready if called home to heaven? Have we fulfilled our purpose on this earth? Is all in order? Thoughts roam around in our heads about our mortality, and reflections become a way of life in isolation. It is uncomfortable, but discomfort is the first sign of a movement forward in our lives. A movement toward justifying our place in this world, in this time and space.

    Such a time calls for warriors and soldiers prepared for battle. It is a time of unrest, unsurety, uncertainty, and trepidation. These times call for courage from the strength of God. So how do we prepare for battle. First, by allowing our hearts to trust God, as Our Commander-In-Chief, the Highest Sovereignty, and most important is to know that His Will shall be done. He is with you encouraging us to connect solely with our faith in Him. We must pray for our world to be rescued, restored and revived to a better place. The uncertainty that we are feeling is change, and change is essential for our well-being. Change is always uncomfortable, and sometimes, it allows us to feel anxious, but once past the hurdle, change can be the direction that He is leading us from our routine, patterned, and mundane lives going nowhere. What we have lost is the truth, we have accepted versions of the truth as we gloss over it with shades of gray. After a while, as time goes forward, it is blurred and lost, never to reach our minds and hearts again. It is then that it becomes a norm, a way of thinking by those whose agenda is damaging to our souls.

A lost world filled with lies. Only by His grace and His wisdom can we prevail.

   Much is at stake, if we continue on this path to nowhere. In this world, we will have tribulation and strife if we stand for the truth. But the truth must prevail at all cost. We must find our way back home to God. Our souls are hungering for the truth and for those who are lost, they will just feel an emptiness, a void which nothing can fill except His Living Word. Every source is available now by His Mercy and Love. All is attainable now in His Graces. His graces abound in great measure to bring this world an answer to its prayers. Rise up and be counted as One of His children void of the doubt and the measures of control enforced upon us. Time is prevalent, do not lose sight of your goal, run your race! This is a time for the second ultimate Plot Twist by Our Almighty Father.

DIVINE MERCY

…before I come as the Just Judge, I am coming first as the King of Mercy…before I come as a Just Judge, I first open wide the door of My Mercy. He who refuses to pass through the door of My Mercy must pass through the Door of My Justice…

On February 22nd, 1931, Sr. Faustina known as St. Maria Faustina Kowalski venerated by Pope John Paul II, Jesus appeared to her and the room became illumined with the most magnificent light. This Chaplet To The Divine Mercy (said on the beads of the rosary) was given to her for the whole world. She was told that at 3:00 p.m., the Holy Hour, is so important because it is the time of Jesus' death on the cross for mercy and forgiveness. Jesus told Blessed Sister Faustina:

The graces of My mercy are drawn by means of one vessel only, and that is – trust. The more a soul trusts, the more it will

receive. Souls that trust boundlessly are a great comfort to Me, because I pour all the treasures of My graces into them. I rejoice that they ask for much, because it is My desire to give much, very much. (V.148). The soul that trusts in My mercy is most fortunate, because I myself take care of it (IV.29). No soul that has called upon My mercy has been disappointed or brought to shame. I delight particularly in a soul which has placed its trust in My goodness" (V.125)

CHAPLET TO THE DIVINE MERCY (I.197)

Introductory:
Our Father... Hail Mary... I believe in God...

On the beads of the OUR FATHER, recite the following words:
V. Eternal Father, I offer you the Body and Blood, Soul and Divinity of Your dearly beloved Son, Our Lord Jesus Christ.
R. In atonement for our sins and those of the whole world.

On the beads of the HAIL MARY, recite the following words:
V. For the sake of His sorrowful Passion,
R. Have mercy on us and on the whole world.

To finish, say three times:
V. Holy God, Holy Mighty One, Holy Eternal One;
R. Have mercy on us and on the whole world.

Jesus to Sister Faustina:

"Let no soul fear to draw near to Me, even though its sins be as scarlet" (II.138)

"I will refuse nothing to the soul that makes a request of Me in virtue of My Passion." (IV.59)

THE HOUR OF MERCY

"I remind you, My daughter, that as often as you hear the clock strike the third hour, immerse yourself completely in My mercy, adoring and glorifying it; invoke its omnipotence for the whole world, and particularly for poor sinners; for at that moment mercy was opened wide for every soul" (V.144).

"This is the hour of great mercy for the whole world" (IV.59)

FULL CIRCLE

In these current times, I have attempted to summarize some of the agenda that is coming against us. I have also spent half of my book providing the means to combat these forces of evil in a spiritual manner, prayers, Our Lord and Savior Jesus Christ, Our Blessed Mother, St. Michael, The Hierarchy of Angels, and finally, the Rosary. I have also included the messages from Our Lady which are powerful in direction and guidance. Make no mistake, there is only one way out, follow God, pray, and strengthen your foundation of faith, hope, and trust.

Believers have been abandoned by those on this earth who should be Our Shepherds. Our churches being closed, no sacraments;, communion, confession, even the last rites to those who are dying, no mass on Easter Sunday, abortion clinics opened for service, crickets from the Vatican, but yet in his book, he criticizes the people about their protest of mask and sides with the government.

"The Pope isn't an absolute sovereign, whose thoughts and desires are law. On the contrary, the ministry of the pope is the guarantor of the obedience toward Christ and His Word."

Pope Benedict XVI – Homily, May 2005

The truth is that our faith is essential, receiving sacraments are essential, going to mass is essential, and living a life of freedom without fear is essential.

"So they were scattered for lack of a shepherd, and became food for all the wild beasts."
Ezekiel 34: 5

"Thus says the Lord GOD: I swear I am coming against these shepherds, I will claim my sheep from them and put a stop to their shepherding my sheep so that they may no longer pasture themselves. I will save my

sheep, that they may no longer be food for their mouths."
Ezekiel 34: 10

"For thus says the Lord GOD: I myself will look after and tend my sheep. As a shepherd tends his flock when he finds himself among this scattered sheep, so will I tend my sheep. I will rescue them from every place where they were scattered when it was cloudy and dark."
Ezekiel 34: 11-12

"I myself will pasture my sheep, I myself will give them rest, says the Lord GOD. The lost I will seek out, the strayed I will bring back, the injured I will bind up, the sick I will heal (but the sleek and the strong I will destroy) shepherding rightly.
Ezekiel 34: 15-1

WORDS OF ENCOURAGEMENT

THE WORD OF GOD:
Our Shepherd – Jesus Christ

"I will make a covenant of peace with them, and rid the country of ravenous beasts, that they may dwell securely in the desert and sleep in the forests. I will place them about my hill, sending rain in due season, rains that shall be a blessing to them. The trees of the field shall bear their fruits, and the land its crops, and they shall dwell securely on their own soil. Thus they shall know that I am the Lord when I break the bonds of their yoke and free them from the power of those who enslaved them. They shall no longer be despoiled by the nations or devoured by beasts of the earth, but shall dwell secure, with no one to frighten them. I will prepare for them peaceful fields for planting; they shall no longer be carried off by famine in the land, or hear the reproaches of the nations. Thus they shall

know that I, the Lord, am their God, and they are my people, the house of Israel, says the Lord GOD. {You, my sheep, you are the sheep of my pasture, and I am your God, says the Lord GOD.}

Ezekiel 34: 25-31

Seek the Truth. Be not Afraid. Pray without ceasing. Be courageous and strong in your faith. Do not stray from the fold. There is where Freedom lies, and Hope is eternal. Use the Sword of the Spirit, His Words from Scripture, to battle against the forces of evil.

"We know that all things work for good for those who love God, who are called according to his purpose."
Romans 8: 28

"If God is for us, who can be against us?
Romans 8: 31

"...in all these things we conquer overwhelmingly through him who loved us.

**For I am convinced that neither death, nor life, nor angels, nor principalities, nor present things, nor future things, nor powers, nor height, nor depth, nor any other creature will be able to separate us from the love of God in Christ Jesus our Lord."
Romans 8: 37-39**

Words of a Shepherd on Earth

Archbishop Carlo Maria Vigano - 'We are not alone': A 2020 recap, December 15, 2020 (lifesitenews.com – Opinion)

Due to the lengthy article, I only included excerpts, please feel free to peruse his writings for spiritual guidance.

… "The months that we leave behind represent one of the darkest moments in the history of humanity; for the first time ever, since the birth of the Savior, the Holy Keys have been used to close churches and restrict the celebration of the Mass and the Sacraments, almost in anticipation of the abolition of the daily Sacrifice prophesied by Daniel, which will take place during the reign of the Antichrist. For the first time ever, at the Easter celebration of the Lord's Resurrection, many of us were forced to assist at Mass and Holy Week services through the internet, depriving us of Holy Communion. For the first time, we became aware, with pain and dismay, of being deserted by our bishops and parish priests, who were barricaded in their palaces and rectories out of fear of a seasonal flu that claimed about the same number of victims as in other years."

"We have seen – so to speak – the generals and officers abandon their army, and in some cases, they even joined the enemy ranks, imposing on the Church an unconditional surrender to the absurd reasons for the pseudo-pandemic. Never, down all the centuries, has so much faint-heartedness, so much cowardice, so much desire to pander to our persecutors found such fertile ground in those who ought to be our guides and leaders. And what most scandalized many of us was the realization that this betrayal involved the highest levels of the

Hierarchy of the Church much more than the priests and the simple faithful. Precisely from the highest Throne, from which we should have expected a firm and authoritative intervention in defense of the rights of God, of the freedom of the Church and the salvation of souls, we have received instead invitations to obey unjust laws, illegitimate norms, and irrational orders. And in the words that the media promptly spread from Santa Marta, we recognized many, too many, nods to the insider language of the globalist elite – *fraternity, universal income, new world order, build back better, great reset, nothing will be ever be the same again, resilience* – all words of the new language, which testify to the *idem sentire* of those who speak them and those who listen to them..."

Last two paragraphs...

...." The Lord will give us the victory only when we bow down to Him as our King. And if we cannot yet proclaim Him as King of our Nations because of the impiety of those who govern us, we can nevertheless consecrate ourselves, our families, and our communities to

Him. And those who dare to challenge Heaven in the name of "Nothing will be the same again," we respond by invoking God with renewed fervor: "As it was in beginning, is now and ever shall be, world without end."

"Let us pray to the Immaculate Virgin, Tabernacle of the Most High, asking that in our meditation on the Holy Nativity of Her Divine Son which now draws near, She may dispel our fear and solitude, gathering us together in adoration around the manger. In the poverty of the crib, in the silence of the cave of Bethlehem, the song of the Angels resounds; the one true Light of the world shines forth, adored by the shepherds and the Magi, and Creation itself bows down, adorning the vault of heaven with a shining Star. Veni, Emmanuel: captivum solve Israel. Come, O Emmanuel, free your imprisoned people."

Again, It is worth reiterating His Word in John 14: 6 during the Last Supper:

"Do not let your hearts be troubled. You have faith in God; have faith also in me. In my Father's house there are many dwelling

places. If there were not, would I have told you that I am going to prepare a place for you? And if I go and prepare a place for you, I will come back again and take you to myself, so that where I am you also may be. Where [I] am going you know the way. Thomas said to him, "Master, we do not know where you are going; how can we know the way?" Jesus said to him, "I am the way and the truth and the life. No one comes to the Father except through me. If you know me, then you will also know my Father."

You Are the Hiding Place From the Wind

This book was written to give status in this present time, and the agenda of evil against the world. It is not to be taken lightly, every word has been provided to battle against such evil forces, in truth and prayer. The time draws near, and we must be able to withstand the storms in our lives. The wind will blow, and we must move with it toward the path designated for each of us in this time and space. Our faith and trust in God will sustain us at this time against such an evil agenda meant to destroy, and wreak havoc on our lives.

So pray for protection, guidance, and the will to persevere and believe that the battles belong to God.

My prayer is that so many will find their way to freedom, and the peace that surpasses all understanding. Only in Him, through Him, by Him, and because of Him can we prevail in this war for our souls.

"From now on I am telling you before it happens, so that when it happens you may believe that I AM."
John 13: 19

St. John Paul II said it is **"the final confrontation between Christ and the antichrist."**

"Because you have kept my message of endurance, I will keep you safe in the time of trial that is going to come to the whole world to test its inhabitants of the earth."
Revelation 3: 10

"I am the Alpha and the Omega, says the Lord God, "the one who is and who was and who is to come, the almighty."
Revelations 1: 8

**A Message from Our Lady in Medjugorje:
   February 15, 1984**

"The wind is my sign. I will come in the wind. When the wind blows, know that I am with you…"

Personal Notes & Final Thoughts

Personal Notes

My writings seem to take me upon the path of eliciting the truth on a spiritual level regarding human nature and the nature of God. I do not presume that I may officiate a pastoral position to guiding souls toward eternity, but, rather, allow them to understand and know the availability of the love and power of God in their everyday lives. In order to do so, I felt inspired to write in this book the prayers and messages that will assist us in this endeavor to become closer to God. The Sword of the Spirit is the Word of God:

"Indeed, the word of God is living and effective, sharper than any two-edged sword, penetrating even between soul and spirit, joints and marrow, and able to discern reflections and thoughts of the heart."
Hebrews 4: 12

No problem is too small and not too great for Him to intercede for us. He is a merciful God, and is forever giving us ways to conquer our human nature by prayer and Scripture. By these weapons, we can fight and defeat that which comes against us.

This pandemic has had and continues to have a debilitating effect upon the minds and hearts of all people, both young and old. Many people losing their jobs, businesses closing, schools closed, remote learning, isolated from loved ones and friends; a complete change to our way of life. This book was my battle cry against the injustices imposed upon us by this world. It is a cry to keep freedom alive in our hearts and souls by the grace of God and to ask for the gift of discernment to know the truth. It is also to remember who we are; we are children of God. We will never be forsaken, but rather, chosen for greatness. We have been called to be a light in the darkness, and never lose hope. If we who know Him fall, who will stand.

"By smooth words he will turn to godlessness those who act wickedly toward

the covenant, but the people who know their God will display strength and take action." Daniel 11: 32

Without faith and hope in God, we will not succeed, because the scales of justice have been tipped too far against us.

"What then shall we say to this? If God is for us, who can be against us?" Romans 8: 31

Final Thoughts

In a world that is hell-bent on destroying or dividing us by identity, we are reaching the pinnacle of unawareness and thoughtlessness. It is no wonder that an array of phrases, words, and the use of pronouns are being infiltrated into our society at a rapid speed, while, simultaneously, applying rules and regulations with a strong dose of fear about this virus. Well done if one's objective is to gain control over a society, and put forth an agenda with cataclysmic proportions upon our way of life.

Like a tsunami, we are constantly being inundated with confusing and ambiguous information, and unable to lift our heads above the water long enough to catch our breath. As a woman, a mother, and a grandmother, my thoughts of the future lie with my daughters and my grandchildren. What legacy are we leaving behind, one of fear and compliancy to those who believe that "they" know better. Or a legacy built on the foundation of faith and trust in God, which will be able to sustain them through the storms in their lives. This foundation is built from the theological virtues (faith, hope, and love) to establish a strong character; one of dignity, integrity, and respect impenetrable against the backlash of intended consequences. He is Our Judge, and how we weather this storm will prove how grounded we are in our faith and trust in Him. We are never alone, He is with us always. Always seek the truth, because there lies our freedom. He is the Way, the Truth and the Life.

On The Wings Of The Wind

www.ingramcontent.com/pod-product-compliance
Lightning Source LLC
Chambersburg PA
CBHW071437070526
44578CB00001B/120